Rhythmic Lead Guitar

Solo Phrasing, Groove, and Timing for All Styles

by Barrett Tagliarino

About the Author

Barrett Tagliarino is a Los Angeles-based guitarist with over twenty-five years of recording, performing, and teaching experience. He's been an instructor at Musicians Institute in Hollywood since 1987, teaching lead and rhythm guitar styles, ear training, theory, and reading. Barrett contributes columns to magazines such as *Guitar Player*, *Guitar Edge*, and *Guitar One*, is featured on the *Classic Rock Soloing* DVD, and is the author of eight music books including *Chord Tone Soloing*, the *Guitar Fretboard Workbook*, and the *Guitar Reading Workbook*.

Barrett has two instrumental CDs, *Throttle Twister* (2009) and *Moe's Art* (1998), showcasing his playing and compositions in a blend of rock, blues, country, and other styles. To buy these and his latest recorded releases, download free tracks, and read his guitar blog posts, please visit his website, monsterguitars.com.

Cover by Ari Baron - www.aribaron.com

ISBN-13
978-0-9802353-2-6

ISBN-10
0-9802353-0-8

Contents

Introduction

The word "rhythmic" in this book's title refers to melodic soloing with a strong awareness of time and phrasing, rather than the rhythm guitarist's job of strumming chords. Both are essential for any working player, but here we'll concentrate on the former.

Soloing books usually teach scales, arpeggios, and chord progressions, and then provide examples for students to copy the timing of notes. This could make you believe you must possess an innate sense of rhythm, when it's actually no different from any other musical topic that deserves attention and study. Many students need work on timing more than anything else, often without their being fully aware of it. The good news is that any timing problem can be fixed in a few months of daily practice.

You don't need to be able to read music before you can use this book. If you are willing to work to tap your foot and count beats aloud, you can get the rhythms right by reading the explanations and listening to the CD. I will explain the standard notation that appears over the tablature a little bit at a time, so you will understand how it works by the time you finish.

To make each lesson as focused and easy as possible, only the necessary background information is given on the spot. Scales, chords, arpeggios, and the fretboard layout are in an appendix at the back for you to review separately from the book's main material.

What You Will Need

A metronome or drum machine or sequencer is required. Even a cheap digital metronome is okay as long as it is loud enough that your recorder picks it up, but don't go without. Every musician needs a metronome.

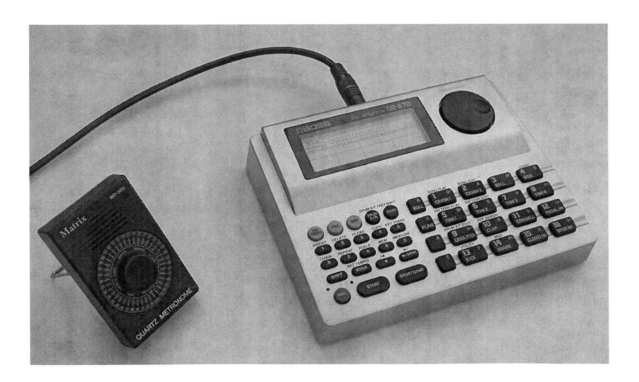

You'll also need a recording device. You can use recording software like Digital Performer or Sonar if you like. Often I just use the built-in mic on a small tape deck or mp3 player/recorder to make quick rhythm tracks, then play them back through my home stereo so I can solo over them.

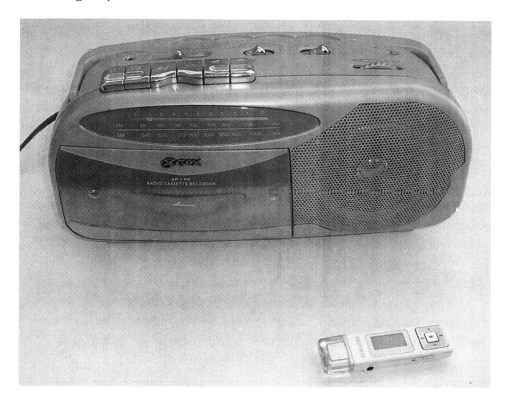

About the Program

As we progress beyond basic beats, timing, and groove, we'll cover syncopation, motific development, phrasing, additive rhythms, and all the odd meters and polyrhythms you are likely to need as a professional. We don't have to go into advanced metric modulations to make interesting music, although by the time we finish you will be able to intelligently attack deeper rhythmic complexity if it interests you. The best course is to get the fundamentals under your belt so you can then go make the kind of music you want.

The early examples are simple and shown in isolation to make sure you can understand them quickly. By the halfway point of the book, some of the concepts are demonstrated with excerpts from my own projects, to help inspire you a little and to reinforce the idea that what you're learning is of practical use. Some of these examples may be a bit too fast to play along with right away, so they're also demonstrated slowly on the CD.

The easier assignments at the beginning of the book will train you to do harder ones that come later, but only if you take your time and don't skip anything—even if one seems trivial. If you think you've found a better way to practice what I'm telling you to do, please let me know about the improvements if you can. Usually when I see this happening, however, it's because the student is misinterpreting the lesson. When in doubt, please trust me and try to do exactly as the instructions say.

If an exercise looks super-easy for you, make sure you can perform it at various metronome settings while counting aloud and tapping your foot, then move ahead. On the other hand, if you run up against one that seems impossibly hard, go back and review the earlier chapters and practice their exercises a little longer. Everything you need is included, broken down into small steps, so if you practice hard, you'll achieve the goal of rhythmic fluency by the end of the book.

Chapter 1: Counting Beats

The object of this lesson is to tap your foot in time with the metronome as you count aloud, then add some picking. I suggest working on this chapter for only ten minutes (but a seriously-focused ten minutes) per practice day, until you meet the standard listed at the end.

Set your recorder down near your foot, start it up, then turn on your metronome set at 60 beats per minute. Keep your heel down and tap the end of your foot on the floor along with each click. If you are a right-handed player, tap your right foot. Use your left foot if you pick left-handed. Tap loudly enough to be heard on the recording.

Tap your foot with the click for at least a full minute, then stop and listen closely to the recording. Notice the foot tap and the click are almost never exactly together. The click is perfectly steady; humans stay in time with it by slightly accelerating or decelerating. This is normal, and the more you practice, the less frequent and obvious your corrections will become.

Now tap the foot along with the metronome as before, and simultaneously count aloud: "one, two, three, four, one, two, three, four," and so on. You are counting beats in a meter indicated by the time signature. The top part of the time signature may be any number and shows how many beats you are counting in each *measure* (also called a *bar*). The bottom number is usually 4, 2, or 8; it tells the type of note you are counting as a beat.

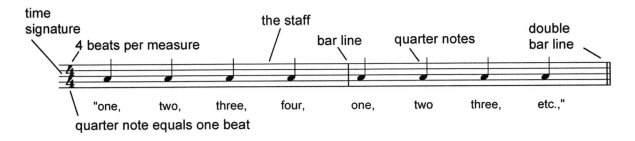

We've got two things going at once now: tapping and counting. Record a bit of this on your own and listen back to make sure you're not skipping any beats in your counting, your foot doesn't drop out, and you're staying in time with the metronome.

Two Kinds of Beats

We use two meanings for the word *beat*. First, each click of the metronome represents a beat as a precise moment in time that has no theoretical duration, just as a point in geometry has a location but covers no area. With this meaning we can say a note begins (attacks) or ends (cuts off) directly on a beat or at some other time in relation to it.

Another meaning of *beat* is the **amount of time** from one metronome click to the next. With this meaning we can say a note is one beat long, half a beat long, two beats long, and so on. If the metronome is set at a slower tempo, the beats are longer.

Quarter Notes

The CD track starts with a two-measure *countoff*, given by a drummer or bandleader so everyone can start together. The traditional countoff for 4/4 time is "one," (rest) "two," (rest) "one, two, three, four." Listen to the countoff and the click **before** you start tapping your foot in time with it.

While tapping your foot, count beats aloud, and play C notes on the 5th string, 3rd fret, right along with the metronome. The notation staff now has a *treble clef* added that determines the pitch of the notes. The 3rd-fret C is on a *ledger* line below the staff in guitar music. There is a *repeat sign* added to the end of the line, telling you to play it two times.

The rectangular marks over the notes are picking directions telling you to play downstrokes only. You're now counting, tapping, and playing the same beats.

CD Track 1

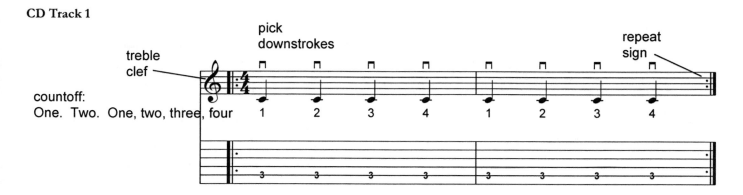

Record yourself playing this exercise and check out how well you stay in time. Especially if you are a beginner, sometimes the only way to get back in sync with the click is to stop playing completely and just listen to it for a bit. That's okay. Dropping out is better than continuing to play *out of time*. When you hear and feel the beat, start tapping your foot again, then add the counting, and finally the playing.

If you are a little more advanced in your playing, notice that often the first bar or two of playing are not quite locked in with the click, after which your groove settles down. You need to really feel the tempo (the speed of the beats) in your body **before** you start playing.

> ### Breathing While Counting
>
> These exercises are meant to be easy enough to let you think about what your body is doing besides playing: tapping the foot, counting, and also breathing. The tendency to hold the breath when playing can mess with your timing and ability to concentrate. It's better to take frequent small breaths and let some air out along with the words as you count aloud. For this chapter's exercises, try inhaling a small breath after beats 2 and 4 in each measure.

Half Notes

The *half note* looks like a quarter note, except its head is hollow. Half notes are always two beats long and can start on beat 1, 2, or 3. Let the note ring while your foot taps the next beat. Keep counting during long notes, so that any following note falls at the right time. You're always counting the beats in the time signature, not the notes themselves.

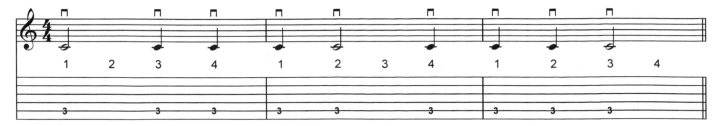

Start Phrasing

Now that we have quarter and half notes, we'll use them to start training your sense of phrasing. A *phrase* is usually two, four, or eight measures. You need to develop a sense of phrase length and play without overlapping it at first. Here we have one and a half measures of quarter notes, then a half note on beat 3 of the second measure. The usual resolution point is about 3/4 of the way through a phrase.

CD Track 2 cont'd.

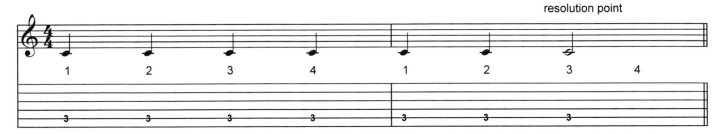

Phrases vs. Motifs

A *phrase* is a complete statement in music, like a sentence or a clause in English. At the end of a phrase there is a sense of finishing an idea and (usually) taking a breath. To find the phrase length in music we look for a chord progression, a figure (or bass riff), or a melody—in that order.

In everyday use the word *phrasing* also refers to how small melodic pieces are arranged over a larger musical context. Technically the phrase is a complete statement defined by the chords, but *phrasing*—and *phrase*—also commonly refer to the smaller licks played over the chords.

A *motif* (or *motive*) is the smallest unit of musical meaning, usually only a few notes. Instead of motif we may use the term *lick, melodic phrase* or even just *phrase* to refer to each solo statement, separate from the phrase provided by the underlying parts.

Whole Notes

A *whole note* is a hollow head with no stem; it's four beats long and always starts on beat 1 of a measure in 4/4 time. Play the example below while counting aloud. The whole note in measure 4 represents a good resolution point for a four-bar phrase.

The whole note in measure 4 may seem like a long stretch of doing nothing, and in the future you may be playing things here. We're learning to feel this as a natural resolution point in the four-measure phrase length. I won't lecture any more now than to say that waiting for the full count of four beats will help you start the next phrase smoothly. This is not the only possible resolution, but it is one to learn early on as a strong alternative to the first beat of the next measure (not shown).

While we have learned three new note durations: quarter notes, half notes, and whole notes, the focus here is on tapping your foot and counting. If you are only playing, there will be problems. Stay with this chapter until you can tap and count quarter-note beats while playing the examples strictly in time with the metronome at slow tempos (50-70 bpm). Record yourself to be sure, especially if you are working without a teacher.

Chapter 2: Beat Division

Eighth Notes

Now we'll **divide** each beat in two parts. Your foot should tap on each beat as before, but now pay attention to how it behaves in between taps. The toe should reach its highest point off the floor exactly midway between metronome clicks.

At that midpoint, you'll strike the string with an upstroke (the V-shaped mark). The pick and tapping foot should move down and up together in a steady motion, like an engine's cycling piston. Say "and" after the beat numbers as shown. You're now counting and playing *eighth notes*, while still tapping quarter notes with the foot. Individual eighth notes have a *flag*; multiple ones may be joined by a *beam*.

As before, train yourself to finish musical phrases at a logical place, on beat 3 of the second measure. Think of the entire two measures as a frame for a balanced picture that includes some space.

CD Track 4

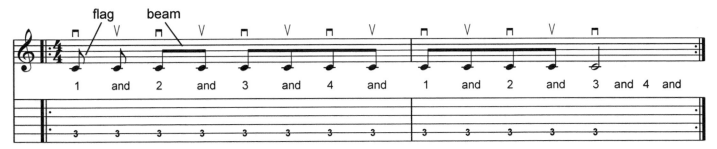

Beat Subdivision: Sixteenth Notes

By subdividing the divided beats, we get *sixteenth* notes, with double beams or flags. As before, tap your foot on the quarter-note beats only, along with the metronome, which should still be set at 60 bpm or slower. As we count through the time more syllables (ees and uhs) are added to represent all the notes. First practice foot-tapping and counting the sixteenths without playing.

CD Track 4 cont'd.

```
Count:     1 e + a 2 e + a 3 e + a 4 e + a
Foot Tap: ↓   ↑   ↓   ↑   ↓   ↑   ↓   ↑
```

Now add sixteenth-note attacks on the C note using steady alternating down- and upstrokes. Keep tapping the foot in quarter notes and counting aloud. If anything drops out, it should be your playing. My students usually must be reminded many times to keep counting and tapping the foot when learning rhythms. No excuses. If you don't learn this before moving on, you're charging into battle with an unloaded gun. If necessary, set the metronome down at 40 bpm so you can count all the subdivisions except for the ones you have to leave out while taking a breath.

Beat Division by Three

When we divide each beat into three parts we get a *triplet*. In 4/4 time this makes twelve notes per bar. Listen and imitate the CD here to make sure your count is evenly spaced.

I've shown two possible ways to pick triplets. For now, use the top method, so you continue to pick down strokes when your foot taps the floor. When playing triplets, there is no correspondence with the upswing of the foot, which should still be tapping even quarter notes as before.

CD Track 5

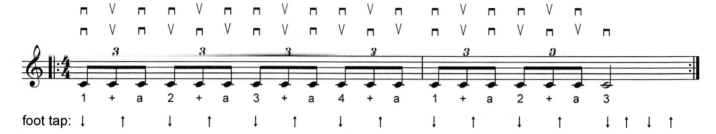

I may omit written beat numbers or divisions where no attacks occur, and count them that way on the CD. But when you or I play through a measure, all the beat and division durations exist whether we count them aloud or not.

The durations are perfectly uniform, even if they appear to be unevenly distributed in the notation. One beat with four sixteenth notes may look longer than a quarter note, but they add up to the same amount of time.

Rhythm Rotation Exercise

1. Here we count measures of quarter notes on the beat, then eighth notes, sixteenth notes, and eighth-note triplets. These four rhythms will become the backbone of your playing. Quarter and half notes are inserted to make the exercise reinforce a natural sense of phrasing.

2. When you can count the various beat divisions reliably while your foot taps constant quarter notes, only then start to play along.

3. When it is consistent, switch to counting only the beats as you play the exercise. The CD track has me counting only the beats while playing all the divisions. The foot taps quarter notes throughout.

CD Track 6

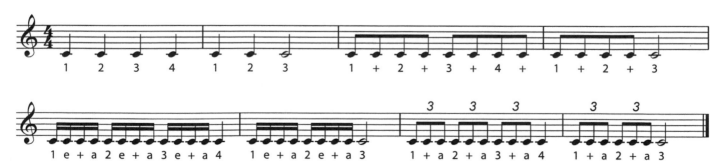

11

Keep those long notes in the exercise for now. If you practice a nonstop barrage, you program yourself to play without regard for your place in the song form.

The rhythm rotation exercise is good for warming up your sense of time and phrasing. Once you can perform it comfortably, change the metronome setting to 80 and try it again. Then move it down to 50. Your goal is to nail each of the four rhythms (quarter, eighth, sixteenth, and triplet) on the first try at any tempo; a skill that will have real-world benefits.

Assignment

Record yourself playing all the examples in this chapter and then listen for rhythmic accuracy. Clean technique can be second in priority to accurate timing for now.

If you have not listened to recordings of your own playing much before, you may have a strong negative reaction to it at first, because you'll hear mistakes you did not notice yourself making at the time. Do not beat yourself up or let the recording discourage you. Instead pick out one small thing that you're going to do better next time

Learning to stay positive and listen constructively to your recordings is a huge step toward becoming your own teacher and making faster progress. Knowing that the microphone is live can help you pay attention and perform better once you are used to it.

Chapter 3: Scales in Time

Scales are good for learning to keep steady time. When well-memorized they become the source for logical melodic choices. In this chapter we'll play a scale along with the metronome, then apply the phrasing principle of breathing space to it. Finally, we'll use a sequence to break up the sound of the pattern and further impress the scale into your memory.

For some of these exercises, we'll count a little differently from before. You'll eventually learn to count many types of units: beats, note groups, bars, sections, and so on. Your foot continues to tap the main *pulse* of the music, so it becomes a rhythmic foundation for whatever you'll play over the top. No matter how long it takes, do the work to master your counting and foot-tapping. You'll enjoy the payoff.

We'll go through two scale patterns in depth, but we won't do it for all of them. I'm relying on you to learn and practice scale patterns on your own. First up is a C major scale in second position. *Position* always refers to the predominant location of your index finger. Shift your index finger to the 3rd fret for the top two strings. The lowest (6th) string, closest to your head, is at the bottom of the diagram.

Unrelated to position, the circled roots on strings 5 and 3 make this Pattern Two in the fretboard system (see the Appendix). We are skipping Pattern One, to avoid its open (unfretted) notes in the key of C, making the upcoming sequence easier to play.

C Major Scale, Pattern Two

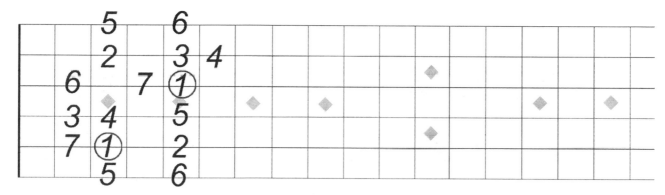

The major scale is the basis for a series of *modes* that can sound anywhere from happy to downright evil, depending on the chord progression or bass notes they are played over. For example, the C major scale above will become A minor if an A bass note is played under it.

C major uses all seven letters of the musical alphabet with no "sharp" or "flat" modifiers: C D E F G A B. We start with the key of C because it is easy to name the notes and describe the scale sequence we'll play. It is useful to also refer to the notes as *scale degrees* 1 through 7, as shown above.

Starting from the C root on the 5th string, practice the scale two ways: first while naming the letters aloud, and then verbally reciting the scale degrees. Both are important. Tap your foot along with the metronome set at 50 and play the scale in eighth notes: two per beat, as shown on the next page.

When the C root on the 3rd string is reached, the numbers and letters start over, though the fingering continues to change. The highest note in the pattern is an A, scale degree 6 in the key of C. When you finish the scale, strum the Pattern Two Cmaj7 chord.

The root of any scale is its "1." That means if we played, for example, a D major scale, the degree numbers would apply to different letters, like this:

D E F# G A B C#
1 2 3 4 5 6 7

Pattern Two on the previous page gives you the D major scale when played in 4th position.

Phrase It

As soon as you can play the above pattern correctly without looking at the diagram, start practicing the scale in a way that reinforces phrasing instincts. We'll make it fit into four measures, which means we don't play every note that is available. This time, instead of naming scale degrees, count the beats in each bar.

CD Track 7

Just running up and down the scale is not a habit you want to form, so as soon as you can do it correctly, start working on variations. Here's your first.

Groups of Four in C Major

Like the scale, this sequence is modified from its most raw theoretical form to support your acquisition of good phrasing reflexes. The first group of four notes is C–D–E–F. Start with your middle finger. This time, only recite the first scale degree of the group, and keep mum during the others.

Now you play another group of four notes, but starting on the second degree of the scale: D–E–F–G. Play the first note of this group with your pinky finger. Start off by saying the word "two" as you play it.

If you've never done this before, go back and practice the two groups in sequence. Memorize it before moving on.

The third group starts on the third degree of the scale: E–F–G–A. This starts with the index finger, and you will speak the word "three" as you begin. Skip "four" and stop with a half note on "five": the G on the 4th string, 5th fret.

By now you may intellectually understand the sequence, but to play it on the guitar while tapping the foot and reciting the scale degree that starts each group is another story. Each group starts with a different finger in a way unrelated to the musical sound except in the bizarre world of the guitar. Take your time and memorize it one group at a time. After a while, your fingers will start knowing where to go.

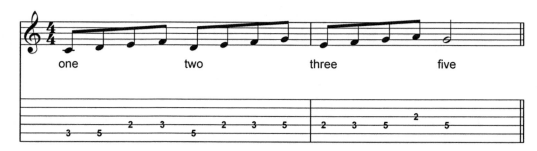

To descend, repeat the G at the 5th fret of string 4 with the little finger. Name these groups by their starting scale degrees: "five, four, three," as you play the four note groups going down the scale. Skip the group that would have started on "two" (D–C–B–A), going straight to the root, C, and name the "one" aloud.

CD Track 8

Groups of Four: The Long Version

Even though we can extend the group-of-four exercise in this position, I still don't want you to start motoring away with an endless stream of notes. There is too much risk you'll stop tapping your foot and become unaware of your location in relation to beat 1 of the measure. Practice should train you for the requirements of real gigs, where keeping your place and fitting into the music is the priority.

With that in mind, here is a longer version of the group-of-four sequence, divided into two four-bar phrases. To make it come out on the downbeat with the tonic note (root) of the scale, we're repeating the highest note. Again, recite the first scale degree of each group.

CD Track 8 cont'd.

When you first learn this exercise, I don't expect you to be able to tap your foot and play it in steady rhythm. It's normal to take a few days if it is new to you. Check out the CD track to hear how my foot taps along with the click while I recite the first scale degree of each group. Record yourself to make sure you're doing the same.

A Minor Scale

The A minor scale shares the same notes as the C major scale. With different roots, the scale degrees all change, too. The fretboard shape made by the circled A roots correspond to the G shape in the CAGED system, making this a Pattern Three minor scale. A minor is the *relative minor* of C, and C is the *relative major* of A minor.

A Minor Scale, Pattern Three

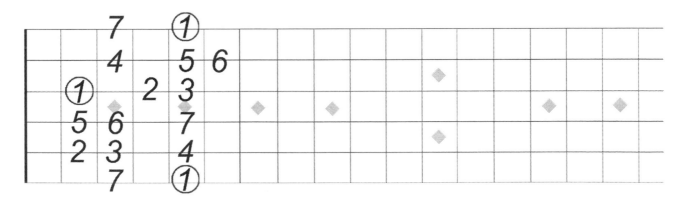

Start from the new root, A, and recite the new scale degree numbers aloud, as you review the pattern. Take notice of the other A roots on strings 3 and 1. Practice it with a quarter-note stop on the high A, to make it fit a pair of two-bar phrases. The A minor 7 chord voicing can be thought of as being common to Patterns Three and Four.

Groups of Four in A Minor

The first group of four notes is A–B–C–D this time. Start with your little finger. Again, recite the initial scale degree of each group. Hold the half note E (degree 5) for two beats, then descend starting from the E, circling and stopping on the low root, A.

CD Track 9

Groups of Four in A Minor, 8-Bar Version

Here's a longer version. Hold out the half notes for their full value at the end of each line.

CD Track 9 cont'd.

Assignment

After taking some time to study the examples in this chapter, record yourself playing each, then listen back and pick out one small thing that you could do better next time. Stay positive. Recordings don't have to be perfect, just better than you played last week. Focus on staying locked in with the metronome, and keeping your verbal count going.

The next chapter does not require mastery of the groups of four, so you can move ahead while continuing to use the sequence in your practice sessions.

Chapter 4: Finding Beats

Quarter Notes and Cutoffs

Tap your foot and count all beats aloud, but only play on the beats indicated in the example. In the first measure, play on beat 1. In the second measure, play on beat 2 only, and so on. **Cut off** each note on the beat that follows it by damping the string. Just like note attacks, cutoffs can have an exact time in relation to the click. Quarter and half rests indicate a silent guitar between tones. The block-shaped half rests are two beats long. They stick up from the center staff line. Practice using single notes, and also play the same rhythm and cutoffs with a C major barre chord. I've shown a slightly-unconventional way I finger this chord to make sure all the notes ring clearly. Use the fingering that works best for you.

CD Track 10

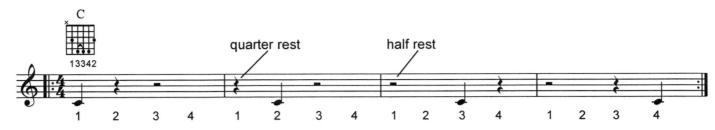

Now make your own series of four quarter-note attack times, and play one per measure on those beats only. Be sure to keep counting and tapping, and wait until the right beat comes along before you hit the note. Cut it off on the next beat. Here's my example: 2–1–4–3.

CD Track 10 cont'd.

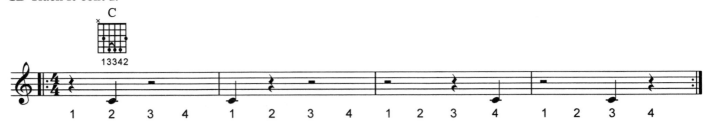

Mark the beats you want to attack here:

     1   2   3   4   1   2   3   4   1   2   3   4   1   2   3   4

Downbeats and Upbeats

Beat 1 of the measure is the *downbeat*. If no number is specified—for example if you only say "hit a note on the downbeat"—then a player will assume you mean beat 1. Beats 2, 3, and 4 are also called "downbeats." Your foot taps the floor for each of them, but for these you have to specify which one you mean. To start my example above I could say "come in on the downbeat of 2."

The *upbeats* are the eighth-note "ands." When talking to other musicians, you'll always have to to specify which upbeat note you want. For example, you might say "play a C on the 'and' of 1." The player will hit a C an eighth note **after** beat 1.

Upbeat Cutoffs

CD Track 11

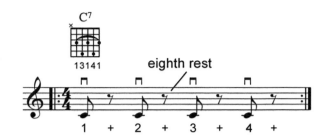

Downbeat eighth notes have the same attack times as quarter notes. Eighth notes are half the duration of quarter notes, so playing them only on the downbeats leaves *eighth rests* on the upbeats. Your upbeat cutoffs should happen when your foot is at its highest point off the floor, halfway between metronome clicks. Your spoken "and" should be heard by itself. Practice the same figure with a chord too. This time make it a Pattern Two C7 chord, voiced 1-5-♭7-3-5.

Upbeat Attacks

Isolating upbeat eighth-note attacks is a little harder than downbeats, so we'll spread out the work and repeat each several times. Play only the "and" of beat 1 for four bars, then the "and" of 2 four times, and so on. Keep tapping and counting.

Pick the upbeat attacks using upstrokes only, with cutoffs on the downbeat. The remaining space in the measure is filled with rests. If you're not an experienced reader, just make sure you hit the note at the proper place above the count, and cut it off right as your foot hits the floor.

CD Track 12

Alternate Pick Movement Even When You're Not Picking

For now, all upbeat notes and chords are to be played with upstrokes of the pick. All downbeat notes and chords should be played with downstrokes. Let your pick hand maintain its constant motion along with the foot, as if you were playing all the eighth notes, but **make the pick miss** the string until the down- or upstroke you need comes along. Learn to pick (and strum chords) this rhythm-oriented way now, before you build up habits you'll have to unlearn later. Alternate-picking motion combats the tendency to rush, and will facilitate your execution of complex rhythms later.

Now we'll play **all** the upbeat eighth-note attacks in one measure. This is often the rhythm guitar part in ska music, so let's make our chord voicing fit that style and play a C major triad on the top three strings only. Make sure you don't let your foot start tapping on the upbeats. It takes concentration and disciplined counting to keep from rushing this rhythm and/or "turning the beat around" with your foot.

CD Track 12 cont'd.

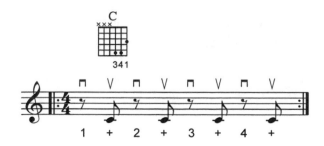

19

Finally, play all four upbeat permutations in a row, in single notes, and with a C minor 7th chord this time. Once you understand the example, try playing it with the metronome only, without looking at the book. Maintain the count with your voice.

CD Track 13

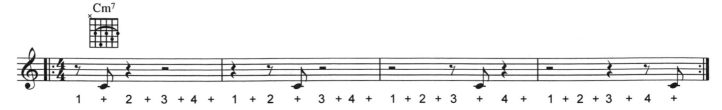

This rhythm figure is a mixture of down- and upbeat eighth notes. Obey the rests and cut each tone off on the very next down or up beat, except in the places where there are consecutive notes. Those particular notes should be hit while the string is still ringing, with no cutoffs in between. Record your playing along with mine on the CD to check for accuracy.

CD Track 14

Only after you start a habit of alternating pick movement for precise rhythmic execution of single-string notes should you dig into other techniques like economy- and sweep-picking. They'll sound much stronger with this foundation.

Assignment

As usual, your assignment is to record yourself playing the examples. If you have access to a video camera, all the better. Watch your picking hand to make sure it is alternating, with downstrokes on downbeats, and continuing to keep time during rests.

The CD for this book is packed full of examples, and most are played very slowly to help you learn and correctly count out the rhythms. Learning to count the various rhythms should be the focus of your study more than memorizing the examples themselves.

Some examples may be too hard for you to play along with the click at first. When this happens stop the CD or your metronome and count the example out one step at a time. Figure out where each note fits in relation to the count and your foot taps. Start playing the example with the metronome as soon as you can.

When working examples up to higher tempos, it will eventually become impossible to enunciate every tiny division without biting your tongue. At that point it is all right to count only the main numbered beats that you are tapping with your foot. The unspoken beat divisions should still be felt clearly in your mind.

Chapter 5: Quarter-Note Syncopation

For syncopation examples we'll play some rudimentary rock riffs on the low-sounding strings.

Strong and Weak Beats

Beats 1 and 3 of the measure are the strong beats. By comparison, beats 2 and 4 are the weak beats. (2 and 4 are also called the back beats.)

```
S W S W
1 2 3 4
```

In this example the pitch changes on strong beats only. Play while counting.

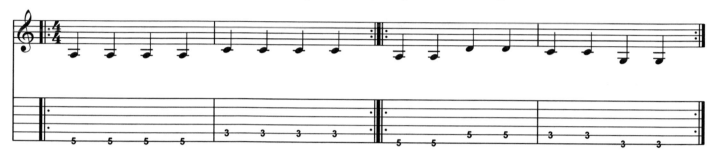

When you move a pitch or chord change that you normally play on a strong beat onto a weak beat, you are performing a *syncopation*. For example, we can change a pitch or a chord a quarter note early, on beat 4 of the previous measure. This syncopated rhythm is a quarter-note *anticipation* or *push*.

Quarter Note Anticipation

CD Track 15

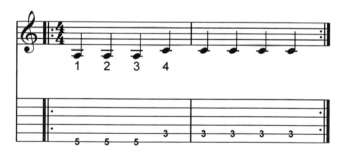

You can hear the guitars play a quarter-note anticipation from the first to the second measure of AC/DC's "Money Talks," while the bass plays steady quarter notes.

Quarter Note Delay

In a quarter-note delay we change repeated pitches or chords a beat **later** than usual, on beat 2 of the measure.

You can hear a quarter-note delay in bar 16 of Stevie Ray Vaughan's instrumental "Testify." Quarter note syncopations have an obvious and powerful impact in the music and can make song arrangements more interesting.

CD Track 15 cont'd.

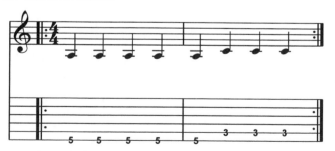

More Long Tones

To make the syncopation effect more powerful, we can let notes ring for longer after attacking them on the upbeats. First let's review the long notes we've played before. The only difference is now we're changing pitch on one of the attacks. A half note starts this measure, followed by a quarter note on the same pitch. The C on beat 4 anticipates the next measure.

CD Track 16

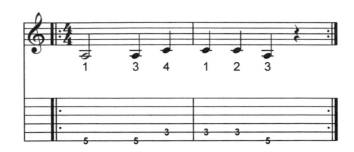

Half notes can come on beat 1, 2, or 3 and are always two beats long. Play these examples while counting aloud.

CD Track 16 cont'd.

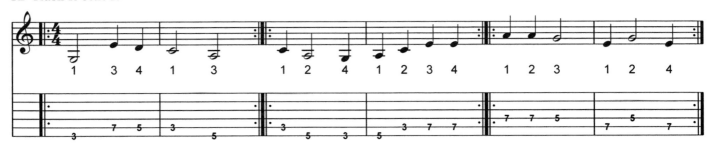

To get all the possible durations and start times, we need to learn two new rhythmic symbols: dots and ties. Nearly all syncopated rhythms can be expressed with just these two symbols and the rests we've seen. Count and play along with the following examples, but take your time. These are a little harder.

Dotted Notes

A dot next to the head of a note makes it longer by half its original value, allowing durations that can't be created with the notes we already know. A dotted half note, then, is equal to a half note (two beats) plus a quarter note (one beat), for a total of three beats of duration. If there is a dotted half note on beat 1 of the measure, anything after it must start on beat 4.

CD Track 17

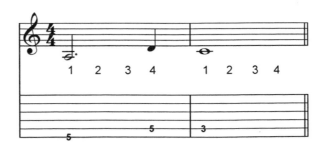

A dotted half note can also appear on beat 2 of the measure in 4/4 time. After this note, there is no more room in the bar.

Tied Notes

CD Track 18

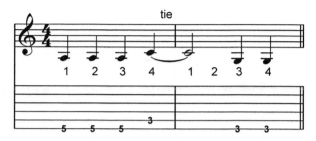

A long note that starts on beat 4 has to be written as a quarter note *tied* to another note in the next measure. When two notes are tied together, only the first one is struck. The next one just adds duration. In this example, the tone is cut off by the attack on beat 3 of the second bar.

Tap your foot and count the four beats of each measure as you hit these notes, and let them ring until the next attack.

CD Track 18 cont'd.

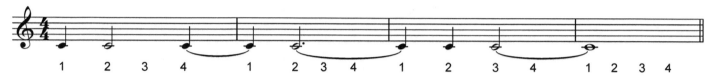

Quarter-Note Syncopation Exercises

Here are all the possible syncopated changes at the quarter-note level, expressed with two pitches. Let the notes ring as you tap your foot and count.

CD Track 19

These 2-bar examples use quarter-note syncopation, a bare minimum of the other note durations we know, and a total of only four pitches, to show in a very basic way how you might work up a rock intro or rhythm figure. Count and play these, then write out one of your own of similar simplicity.

CD Track 20

a.

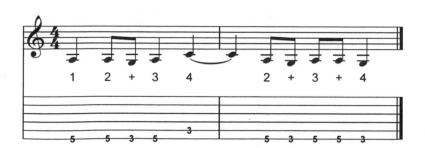

b.

c.

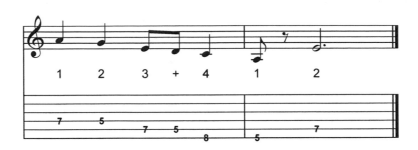

d.

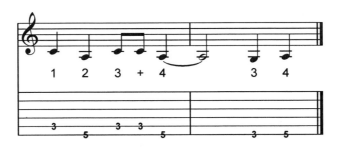

e.

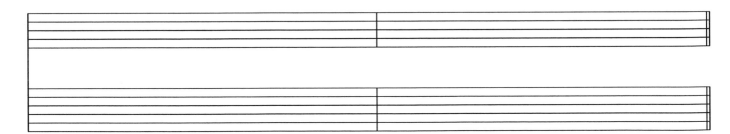

Assignment

Record this chapter's examples with the metronome and monitor your rhythmic accuracy. It would be a nice idea to save some recordings so you can check them out a few months from now to see how your timing has improved. If you're working consistently and with focused intent, you're going to get better. It's a good feeling to acknowledge this, and it just might provide motivation.

Chapter 6: Eighth-Note Syncopation

The upbeats are classified as weaker in comparison to the stronger numbered downbeats.

```
S w s w S w s w
1 & 2 & 3 & 4 &
```

When playing continuous eighth notes you will usually play slightly louder on the strong beats and softer on the weak beats, which gives the music a human feel. The beat descriptors *strong* and *weak*, however, do not always mean loud and soft. One way a syncopated feel is established is by *accenting* a weak beat: playing it louder than the strong-beat notes around it.

> If you play eighth notes at a strictly uniform volume (and uniform duration), you will create a stiff or mechanical feeling. This can be desirable for certain types of music (e.g. metal, punk) and for a temporary effect in any style, but genres like blues, jazz, country, and rock should usually have a looser feel, where strong beats have the louder (and sometimes slightly shorter) notes. A musician should be able to control the amount of variation in note volume and duration at the demand of a knowledgeable producer, who might say "tighten it up" versus "make it breathe more," depending on the needs of the recording.
>
> Unless you think there is a failure to communicate, the above instructions should not usually alter your timekeeping. For that, you should hear commands like "lay back" (play behind the beat), "don't rush" (which means you've been rushing and probably didn't notice it), or conceivably "get on top of the groove" (play very slightly ahead of the beat); or the band could be told that the entire song should be played at a different tempo from the start. Other possibilities are that the tempo gradually changes (*accelerando* or *ritardando*), or that certain sections should be faster or slower than others overall.

The obvious way to create syncopation is to change pitch or chord on the weak beat. Within a measure there are four possible eighth-note syncopations, where we'll attack a new note or chord on the "and" of beat 4, 3, 2, or 1. Anticipating a new chord or bass note on the "and" of beat 4 (an eighth-note push) is extremely common, so it's listed first.

Eighth-Note Syncopation with Two Pitches

CD Track 21

a.

b.

c.

d.

Groups of Two Sequence

Repeating the second note of a scale and every note thereafter creates a pattern where the new pitch always comes on the upbeat. We'll practice it with a stop on bar 4 of a four-bar phrase.

We need to start playing sequential studies in different keys, for variety and for practice finding new keys and playing their scales in position. Where possible also apply sequences to pentatonic scales.

Groups of Two, E-flat Major Scale, Pattern Three

CD Track 22

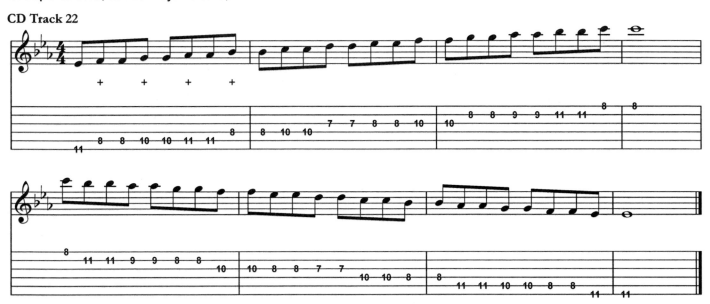

Groups of Two, C Minor Pentatonic Scale, Patterns Three and Four

CD Track 22 cont'd.

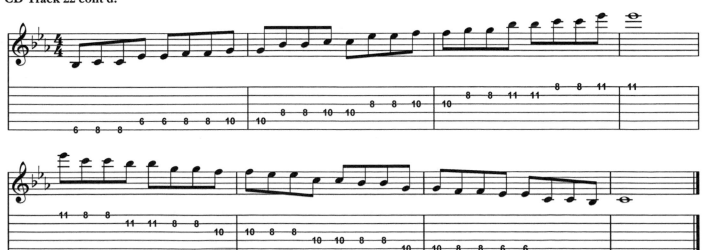

Van Halen's "Ain't Talkin' 'Bout Love" (at 0:20) uses the group-of-two sequence on one string only, sliding up the A minor pentatonic scale.

Dotted Quarter Notes

CD Track 23

A dotted quarter note is equal to a quarter plus an eighth. The dot on the quarter note here occupies an eighth-note's time starting from beat 2. When a dotted quarter note is on beat 1, the note that comes just after it must start on the "and" of 2, and you'd want to play it with an upstroke.

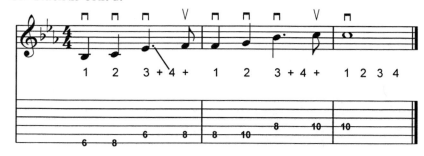

CD Track 23 cont'd.

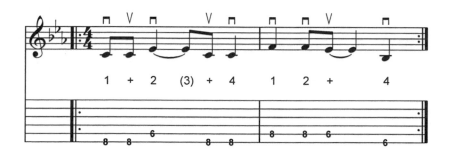

We can have dotted quarter notes starting on beat 1 or beat 3 (or both) within a measure of 4/4 time. Anything directly after a dotted quarter note on beat 3 must start on the "and" of 4.

CD Track 23 cont'd.

A dotted quarter note may be written on the "and" of beats 1 and/or 3. As long as there is something on beat 3, you can keep your place visually. Follow the picking directions.

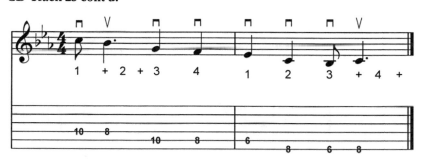

Ties at the Eighth-Note Level

Ties are used when a note with a solid head (a quarter note or smaller) crosses beat 3 of the measure. This means you shouldn't normally see a dotted quarter note on beat 2 in 4/4 time. An eighth note is tied on instead, though the sound is the same: a tone that lasts for one and a half beats. Remember to use upstrokes for any note that falls on an "and."

CD Track 24

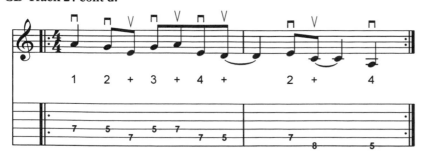

As before, a tie is also needed if any tone crosses the downbeat of the next bar.

More Basic Syncopated Eighth Note Examples

With dotted quarter notes and tied eighths we open the door to an endless supply of rhythmic ideas. Try these out, then write down one of your own, keeping it simple. Start with just one dotted quarter note or a tied rhythm. A little bit of syncopation can go a long way, and too much of it can confuse the listener. In many cases, a pitch or chord change is best placed directly on the strong beat.

CD Track 25

a.

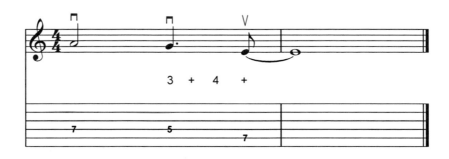

b.

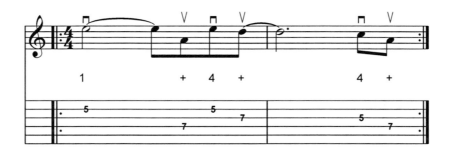

c.

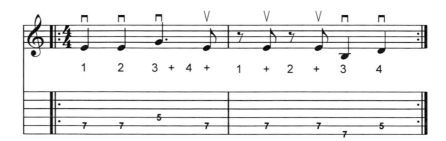

28

d.

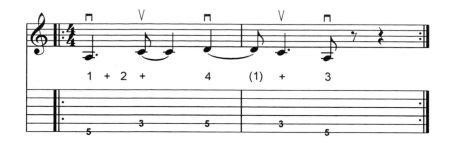

There are rules governing whether to write a tie or a dot that allow the player to keep track of the beats in a measure. If you know the rules for writing music, reading it becomes easier. If you are interested, you can learn the specifics in the *Guitar Reading Workbook*. For this book we are only covering the essentials to support the study of rhythmic soloing; and they are essential. Learn the notation in this chapter well, so you're ready for upcoming material.

Translating the Group of Two into a Syncopated Line

For the earlier group-of-two sequence, or any other where a pitch is played twice in a row, let's practice a version where we make one note include the duration of both. Since the pitch change was on the upbeat, the line has only upbeat attacks now (after beat 1). The modified sequence is shown in B-flat major, Pattern Four.

CD Track 26

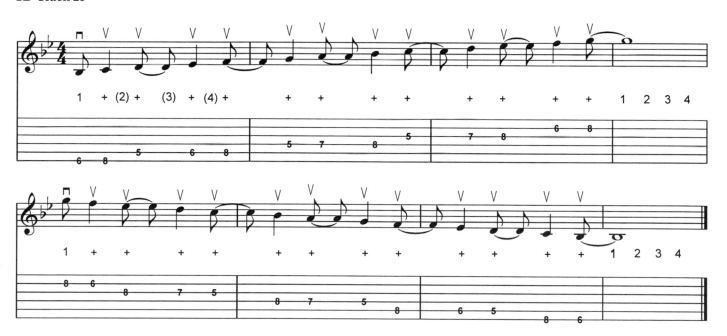

29

We'll also want to practice the tied group-of-two-derived sequence with pentatonic scales. Here it is in A minor.

CD Track 26 cont'd.

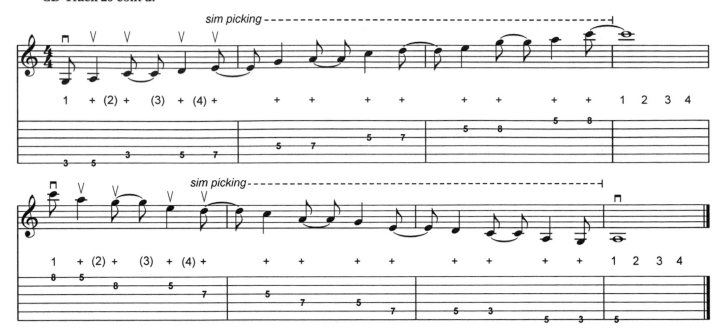

Because the above rhythm is so heavily syncopated, it might sound better if it shifted over to downbeats at the end (as in the bass line of War's "Low Rider"), or if it were used to only introduce or finish a section (as at the ends of the choruses of James Brown's "I Got You (I Feel Good)").

Assignment

Record yourself playing the examples in this chapter. First play them along with a slowly-ticking metronome so you can count the rhythms out aloud. Then turn the metronome up a little and record faster versions. You can drop the verbal counting on the faster version, but you should still be tapping your foot on all the beats, feeling all the beat divisions in your body, and hearing the divisions in your head.

Chapter 7: Pickups

A *pickup* measure is one at the beginning of a song that does not have the full number of beats defined by the time signature. The beginning of a song—and in some cases, the end—is usually the only place this kind of bar may be written. The pickup measure below only contains one beat of music. It contains *pickup notes*, and together those notes are often called a *pickup*. The measure that follows contains the full four beats specified by the time signature.

CD Track 27

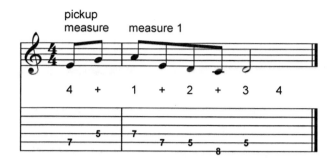

We must practice **counting off** to play a variety of possible pickup lengths, so we can confidently start a song unaccompanied, with the rest of the band coming in later. In the following examples, use the traditional two-bar countoff, but start playing during the second (pickup) bar. These are not really licks that apply to a particular style; they are just important examples of how pickup measures work.

Quarter- and Eighth-Note Pickup Measures

CD Track 27 cont'd.

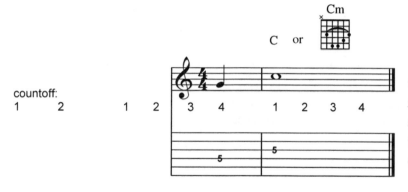

Any tone of the upcoming chord is a good target for a pickup. Here, we're setting up the root of a C major or minor chord with its fifth: a quarter note on G. The fifth of the upcoming tonic chord is one of the strongest pickups you can use in any style from blues to classical.

CD Track 27 cont'd.

Scalar pickups (ascending, or descending as in this example) usually target a tone of the chord on beat 1 of the upcoming measure. This time you come in two beats earlier, on beat 3 in the countoff. Count all the beats in the complete measure too, even if there are only rests at the end. Make it a habit.

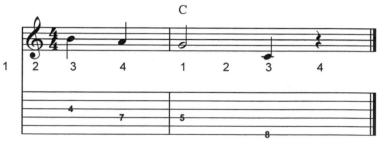

When you have an eighth note in a pickup, start counting "ands" in advance. Use alternate picking here, starting with an upstroke.

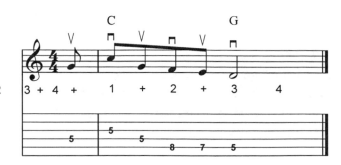

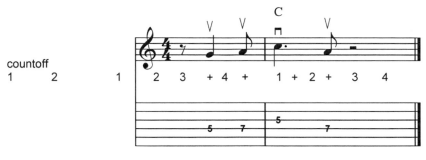

When a pickup contains 3 eighth notes of material, the composer may put an eighth rest at the beginning to help you count and come in correctly.

Rests that appear later in the pickup measure work the same as in complete bars.

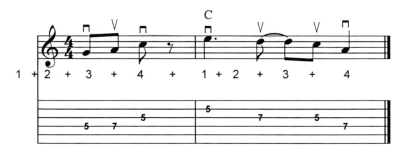

Pickups may be of any length and use any beat division. Pickup bars in the above examples are two beats long or shorter and mostly eighth notes, but you should also try starting earlier in the countoff, and using different note values (including mixtures of note values).

Pickups Can Be Anywhere

Besides the beginning of a song, we can also use the term *pickup* to refer to notes at the beginning of any phrase that "pick up to" the next measure. In the next example, there are a pair of two-measure phrases. The first one starts on the downbeat. The second phrase starts with a one-eighth-note pickup in measure 2.

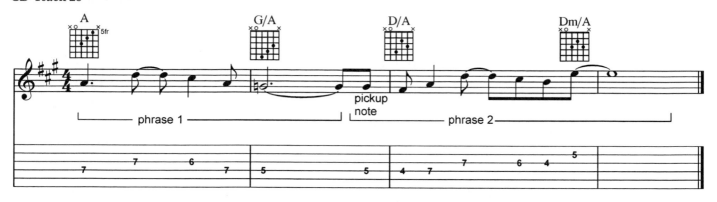

The half- or whole-note pauses we've been leaving at the end of exercises in this book have been training us to leave space for pickups into the next phrase, either our own or those of other soloists in the band.

By working backward from the downbeat you can write out a scalar pickup to any chord tone. With practice you can learn to improvise the same way, reflexively calculating how far away the downbeat is in time and how many pitches are left in the scale before you hit the target tone. Giving your playing this sense of momentum from bar to bar is a skill important enough to merit its own book. *Chord Tone Soloing* drills your reflexes to target all possible chord tones in any progression with scalar movement. If you perform its exercises according to the instructions, they will also sharpen your time awareness.

3/4 Time

In a *triple meter*, your foot taps three times. A traditional 3/4 time-signature song is called a *waltz*. In it, the 1 is still the strong beat; beats 2 and 3 are both considered weak beats. Since a dotted half note lasts for three beats, it takes up a full measure in 3/4 time.

The principles of phrasing we learn for 4/4 also apply to other time signatures. Here is a pentatonic scalar sequence in 3/4 time, with breathing space at the end of the phrase. Make sure your countoff is in 3/4, and that you continue to count in 3/4!

CD Track 29

Here the previous pickup examples are adapted to 3/4 time. Short pickup phrases should usually work in any time signature as long as they're started the correct distance away from the downbeat.

CD Track 30

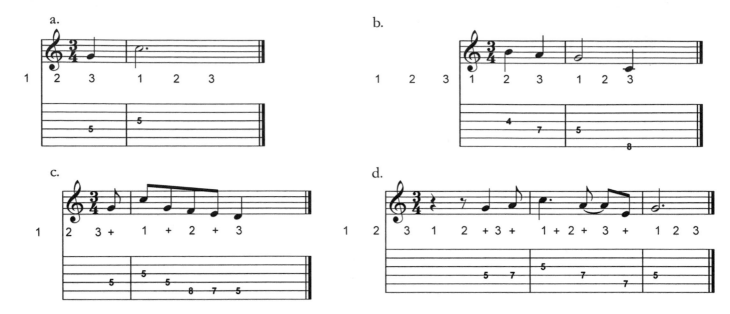

Ants in Your Pants

If you're itching to build up your speed and stamina while still learning to keep your place in a phrase, try replacing the half-note resolutions in the group-of-four sequence with pickups. The resolution points are still heard, and the four-bar phrases are still felt, but the pickup lines let the assault continue. These are groups of 4 in A major, Pattern 5. If you know the scale, you really only need to look at the beginning and end of each line.

CD Track 31

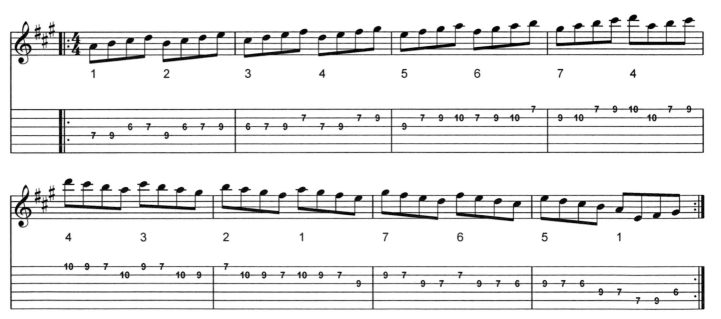

Assignment

Make sure your verbal countoffs are heard as you make your own recordings of the examples in this chapter, and that the pickups come in on the correct beat as written.

Chapter 8: Triplet-Based Rhythms

Eighth-Note Shuffle

By removing the middle of the three attacks in a triplet (the "and"), we get a *shuffle* rhythm. The attack may be removed by using an eighth rest, but it's more often written as a quarter and an eighth note (even when the former rhythm is actually played), bracketed with a "3." The shuffle is a mainstay of the blues, and is present in most styles.

Count and play the triplets and shuffles while tapping the foot in steady quarter notes as usual. Don't let your foot copy the triplet or the shuffle rhythm. Keep it steady and count all three divisions of the beat aloud.

CD Track 32

CD Track 32 cont'd.

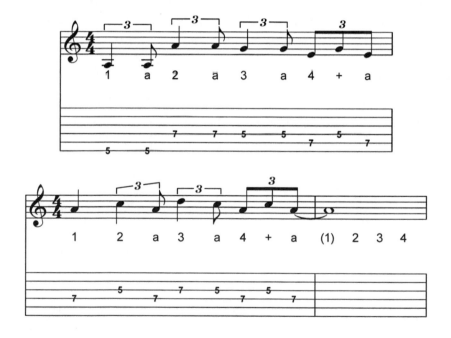

We'll learn more triplet-based licks for these styles in the next chapter, after covering grace notes, slides, and string bending.

Reverse Shuffle

A reverse shuffle is a triplet with the **third** attack removed. This important rhythm may be a bit tricky at first. Listen to the CD, and count aloud. A monotone demonstration is followed by two simple blues licks that use the reverse shuffle.

reverse shuffles

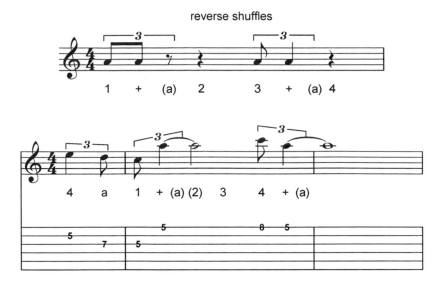

Syncopated Triplets

Ties added to triplets and shuffle rhythms create new combinations of syncopated accents. These can be tricky to play, so we'll just keep them on a single pitch for now.

CD Track 33 cont'd.

The Quarter-Note Triplet

The quarter-note triplet (bar 4 below) spreads three notes evenly across two beats. It's based on two eighth-note triplets (bar 1), but we only attack every other note (bar 2). Then each attack gets a duration of two eighth notes out of the original triplets (bar 3).

CD Track 34

Practice each beat of the quarter-note triplet by itself, making sure the foot taps evenly and that you're feeling every triplet eighth. When both beats are comfortable, join the two one-beat figures.

Playing the quarter-note triplet with your hands while your foot taps in even quarter notes creates a *polyrhythm*: three notes on the top spread evenly against two on the floor. Don't try to guess or fake your way through this rhythm, and don't let the foot tapping deviate from steady quarter notes. Take your time with it.

For an example of a repeated quarter-note triplet, listen to the end of the Doors' "Love Me Two Times," while tapping the foot in 4/4. Learning the song can help you remember the feel of this very common figure.

Compound Meter

When a song or section contains mostly triplet-based rhythms, the notator can do away with all the 3s and brackets by using a *compound* meter, where each beat is divided into three eighth notes instead of two. Common compound meters are 6/8 (two beats per measure), 9/8 (three beats per measure), and 12/8 (four beats per measure). In compound meters each beat is a dotted note.

The sound of these two examples is the same. One is notated in 4/4 (not compound but a *simple* meter), and the other is notated in 12/8 (a compound meter) to make it easier to read. The foot tap and count are the same for both. You don't have to tap your foot twelve times. In any compound meter, you'll tap the dotted-note beats.

CD Track 35

Swing Eighth Notes

When played at slow tempos, a *swing* feel divides the beat the same as a slow blues shuffle. The first eighth note lasts for 2/3 of the beat, and the next eighth note takes the other 1/3. The difference between a shuffle and a swing appears at medium to high tempos. The shuffle continues to divide each beat evenly into three parts (though only the first and third division are attacked) at any metronome setting. In the swing feel, the higher the tempo, the more the ratio between the two eighth notes moves from 2:1 toward 1:1 (evenly-spaced or *straight* eighth notes). At very high tempos the eighth notes are completely even. In other words, the faster the tune, the less the amount of swing.

The CD example shows an easy pentatonic riff played at slow and fast tempos, first shuffled, and then with swing feel. Strictly read, the value assignment over the music states that eighth notes are to be interpreted as triplet shuffles. Though sometimes the same equation is used for swing examples in books, the only way to be sure a swing feel is used on a song is to write *swing, jazz,* or *bop* over the music.

CD Track 36

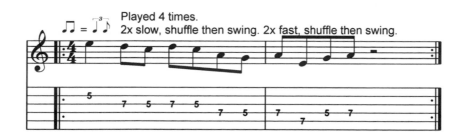

A common mistake made while learning to improvise in the swing feel is playing too many triplets. These should only happen occasionally. This problem goes along with leaning too far in the shuffling direction generally. Once you have learned to consistently maintain a swing feel that approximates a shuffle, try playing your swing lines a little bit straighter than you might expect. Listen to the players you like and imitate their feel.

> The term *swing* also 1) dictates specific parts played by the drummer and bassist, and 2) is used to describe the feeling that a player or an entire band is executing jazz in a rhythmically-appealing way overall. The expression "they're really swinging" can mean they're farther away from a triplet feel than less-accomplished players might be at the same tempo.

Practice descending scales in swing eighth notes. Start on the 2nd degree to resolve to the tonic on the downbeat of the next measure. Add one more eighth note on the 5th degree for a traditional ending to the line. Besides these two examples, also play descending scales like this in other fingering patterns, and in higher or lower octaves where you can.

CD Track 37

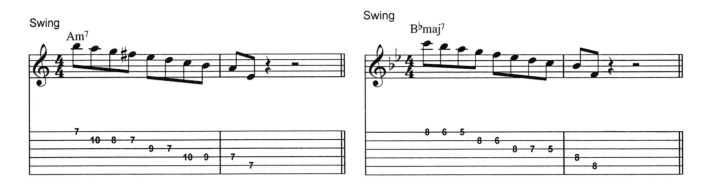

Now swing the eighth notes in 3/4 time: a jazz waltz feel. First learn the typical accompaniment pattern for the chords.

CD Track 38

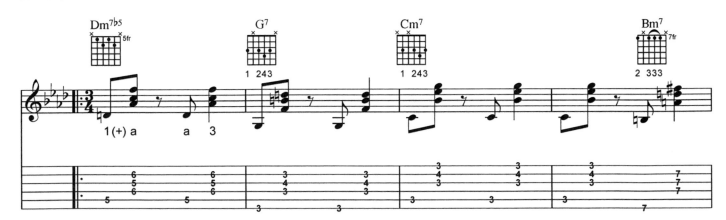

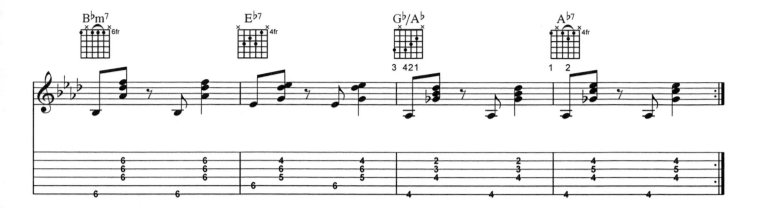

Here's an easy swing eighth-note line to go over the chord changes.

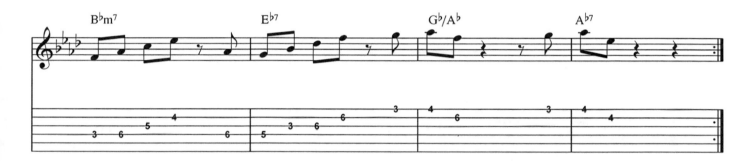

The choice of notes can also contribute to the sensation of swing. Basic jazz lines place dissonant tones on the weak beats to create tension, resolving it with a tone of the current chord on the strong beats. This book is rhythm- rather than chord-oriented, so I won't go into the topic further than saying all aspiring professionals should learn to play scales (and chords) with the swing eighth note feel. Having a grasp of swing doesn't instantly make you a lounge lizard. The swing feel also happens in blues, country, rockabilly, and pop ballads.

Tuplets

The *duplet* may appear in a compound time signature like 12/8. It tells you to go back to playing two evenly-spaced eighth notes per beat, which can be hard to do if you're locked into the feeling of three notes per beat. Practicing the rhythm rotation exercise from Chapter Two can help.

1   +   a   2 (+) a   3   4   and

In most odd tuplets, you are usually compressing notes into a space that was formerly occupied by fewer (the duplet above is an exception). For example, a *quintuplet* is five notes evenly spread across the space normally occupied by four notes of the same denomination. The easiest to feel and execute is the sixteenth-note quintuplet: five notes in one beat. You can just say the word *university* for each metronome click.

CD Track 39 cont'd.

1   2 ni ver si ty 3   4 ni ver si ty

Sixteenth-Note Triplets

A sixteenth-note triplet has three evenly-spaced notes in the space formerly occupied by two sixteenth notes, the same overall duration as one eighth note. One way to count sixteenth-note triplets is by saying "ta ta" after the "and" or the beat number.

CD Track 39 cont'd.

1   +   ta ta 2   3 ta ta +   4

CD Track 39 cont'd.

1 ta ta + ta ta 2   3 ta ta + ta ta 4

You can play two sixteenth-note triplets in one beat: one starting on the downbeat, and one starting on the upbeat, when your foot is at its high point, for a total of six notes in one beat. When there are two sixteenth-note triplets in the same beat like this, sometimes they are notated as a *sextuplet*.

Groups of Three in Triplets

This pentatonic sequence underlies many old-school rock solos. Zeppelin's "Good Times, Bad Times" comes to mind.

CD Track 40

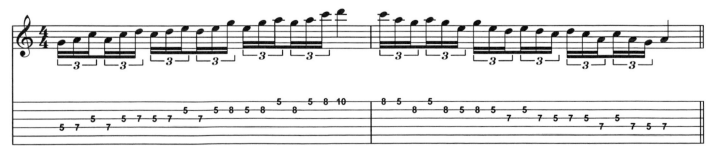

Start any exercise that you practice regularly on one of the guitar's four high strings, not on the lowest string. You want your reflexes to put you in the correct register when it's time to improvise a solo.

Sixteenth-Note Shuffle

The sixteenth-note shuffle works the same as the eighth-note shuffle. The middle attack of a triplet is removed. There's an eighth note followed by a sixteenth note, bracketed with the number 3. A metric assignment over the music states how the sixteenth notes are interpreted. This rhythm feel is used in Toto's "Rosanna" and in some reggae songs like Bob Marley's "Stir It Up." A sixteenth-note shuffle is also called a hip-hop groove or a funk shuffle. Sometimes the term *sixteenth-note swing* is used for it, although sixteenth-note swing technically should be an in-between feel. The two measures sound the same in this example.

CD Track 41

Assignment

Count through the examples in this chapter without the metronome at first. Take your time to say every beat and division aloud, and see how it will align with your foot. It's best to go slowly and get it right. Then record yourself playing the examples with the metronome set slow enough that you can count the beat divisions aloud.

Chapter 9: Articulations

When learning any lick in this chapter, count yourself in as usual so the lick starts and ends on the correct beat. Count through the complete bars, including rests. Never try to save time when practicing by dropping beats out. That would build a bad phrasing reflex.

Articulation means the way a tone is attacked. On the guitar we have multiple articulation possibilities. After striking a fretted note with a pick or finger, we can then bend, slide, hammer on, or pull off to a different pitch. The result is a legato (connected) attack on the second note.

The right articulations make your playing more interesting and convey stylistic consistency. For example, a traditional jazz guitarist might pick on the upbeats and use hammer-ons and pull-offs to slur onto the downbeats for a syncopated swing feel. The *slur* is a curved mark resembling a tie that connects notes of different pitch.

CD Track 42

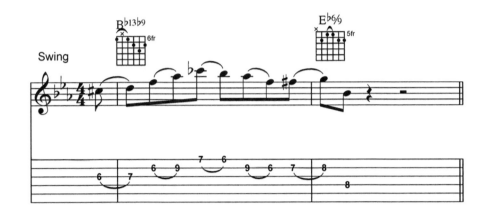

Each type of articulation needs to be assimilated into practice with the metronome so that the timing is still strong. Slurred notes may have a tendency to be rushed or uneven because the picking hand is no longer in control. With most of the articulations, the fretting hand has to do the job of locking in with the metronome by itself.

Briefly practice these exercises, just hammering on and pulling off in time with the metronome, making sure to use all four fret-hand fingers.

Make sure the unpicked notes are played in time in this legato rock lick. I like to use my 4th finger for all the notes on the 8th fret, but you may decide to stretch up with the 3rd finger.

CD Track 43

Slides

When sliding from one fret to another, plan which finger will execute the slide so that you don't run out of fingers for later notes. I like to start the next example with the middle or ring finger. The lick uses definite one-fret and two-fret slides to reinforce control and timing. A slide covering a greater distance in the same amount of time must be faster to keep the destination note on the beat.

CD Track 44

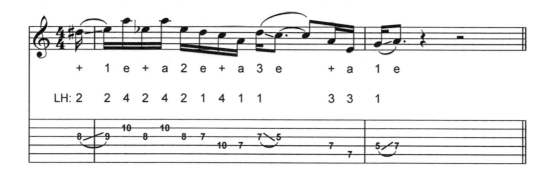

Sliding phrases using a pair of strings are good practice for opening up the fretboard and connecting scale patterns.

CD Track 44 cont'd.

Grace Notes

While the regular notes in a bar must all add up to the time signature, we can add a smaller *grace* note before any of them. The grace note must be fit in (the Italian is *acciaccatura*, "crushed") so the destination note after it falls in its correct rhythmic place. A grace note should be very short. To make sure you nail the attack time of the main notes, leave the grace notes out when learning a new lick at first.

On the guitar, a grace note is usually used as a starting point for a slide or legato attack on the same string. In other words, the main note is seldom picked. One exception is when grace notes on consecutive strings are executed with sweep-picking: a *rake*. Grace notes abound in the blues, so I'm using blues licks in C for demonstration.

CD Track 45

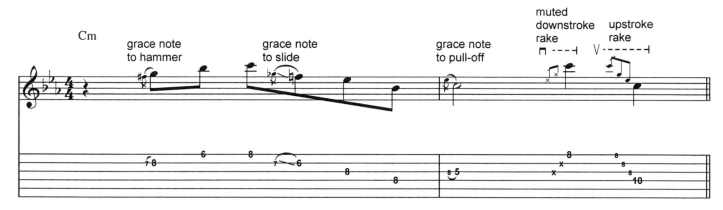

Because grace notes have to start a tiny bit early to let the following note stay in time, learning to execute them takes repetition and patience. Practice counting steady time even when using grace notes, as in the next example.

Reversed Groups of Four

In this exercise we'll kill two birds with one stone, adding grace notes to a new sequencing variation on a C minor scale in Pattern 3. Tap the foot as usual. Name the scale degree that starts each group aloud to help keep you from skipping any groups by mistake. The sequence goes like this:

   4321 5432 etc. on the way up,
   4567 3456 etc. on the way back down.

When you get the sequence figured out, go back and add in the grace notes. Keep the main notes on their written beats.

CD Track 46

Assignment

Work out reversed groups of four on a D major scale using any pattern except Pattern 2 (that's the same fingering as a Pattern 3 minor scale, which we just used). Follow the above example and put in a breathing space, then descend. Find a way to resolve on beat 3 of the last measure. When you have it figured out, add the occasional grace note and connect some of the notes with legato technique.

Bending

Practice these licks with the metronome, and listen closely for accurate timing and bend intonation (correct pitch of the bent string).

CD Track 47

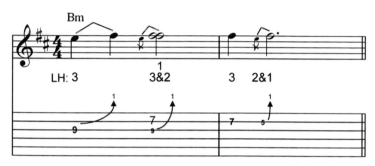

Make sure your bends are in tune by checking them against an unbent note on the same destination pitch. Two strings ringing together form a unison bend. You can also listen to the destination pitch, then follow it with the bent note on the same string (meas. 2). Support the bending finger with another one on the same string a fret lower when possible, and brace your thumb on the top of the neck. Return your thumb to the back of the neck for regular playing.

CD Track 47 cont'd.

There are two main ways to finish a bent note. Make sure you intend one way or the other, so you don't get something in between. The first way is to damp the note completely before relaxing the bending fingers. Here's the same lick in Patterns 4 and 5 of B minor. Don't let the bent pitch drop off before you damp the string.

CD Track 47 cont'd.

Another way to finish a bent note is to return it to a specific lower, unbent pitch. The bend release is a type of articulation for the note that follows and should be a division in time with the metronome, or a well-executed grace note. This lick has a release from F♯ to E in steady eighth notes, then a grace-note release on beat 4.

The most familiar bending licks are in Pattern Four of the minor pentatonic scale. These are whole-step (two-fret) bends from the 4 to the 5, from the ♭3 to the 4, and the ♭7 up to the root.

CD Track 47 cont'd.

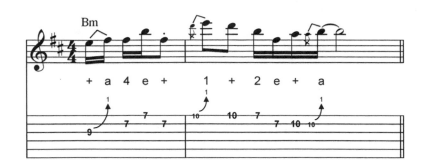

The notation for a *pre-bend* shows the pitch of the unbent note at the same fret in parentheses; the tablature shows a vertical arrow. The bent string is under greater tension and feels different from the same note played elsewhere. The next note is usually the unbent one on the same fret, with or without an audible release.

CD Track 47 cont'd.

Check out the bends between all the degrees in any scale. Each fingering pattern of a scale presents its own possibilities that may be only practical in that position. This lick uses Pattern 3 of a B blues scale variation with a major 6th (G♯). Bent notes in the blues may be less rhythmically precise, slower, and more emotional, but should still reach the intended pitch.

CD Track 47 cont'd.

Bent notes in some traditional country licks emulate the sound of the pedal steel guitar. They should sound mechanical, so bend with even eighth notes straight up to the pitch. In many cases you hold the bent note while you play another note on a different string. Held bends are notated the same as pre-bends, with parenthetical grace notes and vertical arrows. In this example I've placed suggested left-hand fingering on the top.

CD Track 47 cont'd.

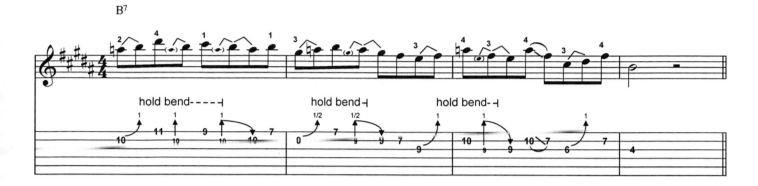

Combined Articulations

Different articulations can be used in rapid succession or even simultaneously on the same pitch. I'll give an example that combines half-step bends and releases with legato technique.

• First pick a note the normal way, fretting it with your 3rd finger.

CD Track 48

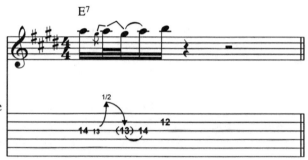

• With the 2nd finger, play the note that is one fret lower, and immediately bend it up a half step.

• So far you have heard the same pitch twice, with the second one being the result of a bend.

• Now release the bend while hammering the 3rd finger back down without picking.

The result is the same pitch three times in a row, but each with a different type of attack; picked, bent, and then a hammer-on as the bend is released. It's written with a 32nd note for clarity but it's two nearly simultaneous actions on the same pitch. To finish the beat, add a B on the 2nd string.

Here's a typical lick combining bends, releases, and hammer-ons.

CD Track 48 cont'd.

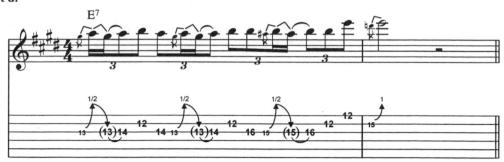

47

Assignment

Write a pentatonic lick with a combined articulation consisting of a whole-step pull-off and an immediate slide back up to the starting pitch. Use any rhythm you like for the main notes of the lick.

Vibrato

Vibrato, created by slightly bending and releasing the string in a regular cycle, should generally be slower when tempos are slower, but it does not have to be in a direct rhythmic relationship to the groove. Even so, you should practice executing vibrato in time with a metronome to learn to keep it smooth and even. The overall speed and width of your vibrato is a stylistic choice. Most inexperienced players should slow down their vibrato a bit to keep it from sounding nervous or erratic. Some situations require a sound with little or no vibrato at all; for example, when harmonized lines from multiple instruments must blend.

The string should return to the starting pitch in each cycle of movement so it sounds in tune. For bent notes this can be a challenge. Hold the bent note up, then release it a bit so it goes slightly flat, then push it back up there. Repeat steadily.

The use of vibrato should be a conscious choice until you have developed the ability to include it only at the appropriate times. You could practice placing vibrato on every other long note of the sequencing exercises in this book.

The decision to include any decorative elements is not automatic, so you should practice **making the choice** to include them or not. Anything you do regularly can easily become a habit that pops out in your improvisations. If you practice strong phrasing in the right register, notes with well-timed articulations, and tasteful vibrato in stylistically appropriate places, that's what you will eventually get.

But if you use vibrato on every note that is long enough to take it, vibrato will appear in places where it does not belong. If you rake into the first note of every lick, you'll find it hard to stop. If you practice playing nonstop scales always starting from the sixth string, you will tend to automatically do that when it's time to solo. If you practice mistakes, you will make mistakes.

While we're on the subject of programming reflexes, it's a good time to say that scales, sequences, and even licks are only a means of developing basic techniques and connecting your fingers to your brain. They are not solos or melodies. Use them for warmups and to learn where the sounds you hear in your head are going to be, but don't stop there. Keep going until you're making real music.

Before proceeding, take time off to review all the rhythmic units presented in the previous chapters, from whole notes down to sixteenth-note triplets, so you can count and play them from memory and identify these rhythms when you hear them.

Chapter 10: Feeling the Groove

You are just as much a contributor to the groove when you are playing lead guitar as when playing an accompanying part. As a soloist you should normally express the same rhythmic precision, only now you're playing melodically with notes of varying length, adding embellishments like slides and vibrato, and including spaces to create the top layer of the arrangement.

For any song or section you'll play over, listen for the smallest recurring division of the groove (not the drum fills) in the hi-hat or ride cymbal part, if one is being played. Next check out the kick drum pattern, the bass guitar part, and then all the other rhythm instruments. Usually the smallest regular part of the groove is an eighth or sixteenth note. You must determine whether this note is played with a straight feel, with a triplet-based or shuffle feel, or with swing feel. If you're not sure, try playing some of the different divisions with your guitar at a low volume while tapping the pulse and listening closely to the other instruments.

Well before you start playing, make sure your foot is tapping the pulse, and make sure you're **already** feeling the smaller division in your body, so you could start counting it aloud at any time. Even if your solo does not consist of notes in that smallest division, you should still be aware of and reflect it as you play. For example, if the drummer is playing straight eighth notes, no one else in the band should normally be shuffling them, except as an intentional effect to create tension.

Exercise 1

Listen to the beginnings of CD tracks 51, 62, and 67. Tap your foot on the quarter-note pulse, then write down the smallest recurring division of the quarter note, and whether the groove is straight, shuffled, or swung for each track. Exercise answers are at the back of the book.

	Beat Division	Feel
51:		
62:		
67:		

Exercise 2

Listen to three recorded songs in various styles and perform similar groove analyses. Find and tap the pulse while counting aloud, then identify the beat division, and whether it is straight, shuffled, or swung. Don't be disappointed if you are not always successful, because it's possible you picked a piece of music that was played with special rhythmic instructions or even played without concern for rhythmic cohesion.

Song	Beat Division	Feel
1. The Who, "Long Live Rock"	eighth note	straight
2.		
3.		
4.		

Rhythmic Options

You may decide to play most of your notes at a different division level from the band in your solo for contrast. If the band is busy with a lot of sixteenth notes, for example, depending on the style you might decide to use mostly eighth notes and larger. If the groove is more spacious, with lots of quarter notes in the bass and drum parts, it may feel right to use eighth notes, triplets, or sixteenths in your solo.

As you work with the metronome, you'll get an idea which notes are within your reach for various tempos. For example, at 120 beats per minute, you may know that you can play continuous eighth notes with no problem, steady triplets are possible as long as they are in a lick that you've practiced a bit, and maybe sixteenth notes are too fast for you to pick, but you might still play some by using hammer-ons and pull-offs, along with some isolated picked sixteenth-note attacks included among longer durations. It's a good idea to write down the tempo at which you successfully performed and recorded any current material on your practice list.

When improvising a solo with other musicians, you may not always know the exact tempo of a song. Your state of preparedness can vary depending on how much you've been practicing recently, whether you are warmed up, and so on. Start with melodic ideas that are well below your technical limits, so that you can be sure to hit the groove from your first notes, and to give yourself room to move into more complex ideas later. Estimate in your head what eighth notes, triplets, sixteenth notes (or smaller, if it's a slow-tempo song) would sound like against the groove before you begin. Depending on the song, your entire melody may consist of long notes and be perfect. The idea is not to figure out how many notes you can jam into a bar but to know which beat divisions are possible, so that your playing contributes to the groove rather than disrupting it.

Exercise 3

Again briefly using CD tracks 51, 62, and 67, tap your foot along with the pulse, counting the quarter note beats, and scratch different note attacks on damped strings: quarter notes, eighth notes, eighth-note triplets, etc., against each. Write the determining division of the groove for each track, then which divisions you think would be within your ability to play.

	Main Beat Division and Feel	Available Beat Divisions for Soloing
51:		
62:		
67:		

Applying Feels to Raw Material

We'll adapt two new pentatonic exercises from a simple (two notes per beat) to a compound (three notes per beat) groove. This is practice for working out how to make a line come out in a logical place so you can apply it in real music. You can do it by counting aloud as you step through the sequence and rearranging some of the notes, especially those at the end of the phrase. It's also a great idea to use pencil and paper.

Descending Groups of Five

These sound especially good when played with solid clear technique. My students enjoy learning, practicing, and using them in solos. In this guitar-specific sequence we'll skip every other group and play only the groups that start with left-hand fingers 3 or 4. This creates an opportunity for consecutive downstrokes between adjacent strings when starting a new group: *economy* picking.

CD Track 49

Descending Groups of Three and Five

This example starts off with a group of five, but the real pattern of alternating groups of three and five starting from the same note begin on beat 3 of the first bar. Reposition the pick during the pulloffs. The economy-picked downstrokes connecting the note groups are not two separate small strokes but rather one larger stroke with an interruption. Push the pick through one string and let it fall directly on the next one: a rest stroke. Push the pick through the next string without rushing the time. Work these up to a brisk tempo, but keep it clean.

CD Track 50

Assignment

For a few minutes of your daily practice routine, review any sequence from Chapters 6-9 originally presented as eighth notes and work it out in triplets (or vice versa). The uneven groups create less-predictable patterns of syncopated accents. Work out a way to finish them on or near beat 3 of bar 2 in a two-bar phrase or beat 1 of bar 4 in a four-bar phrase. They give you more ways to practice picking and timing, drill your scale shapes, develop the ear-to-fingers connection, and gain control of your articulations.

Adapt the licks from Chapters 8 and 9 to fit other contexts, too. If you have a lick that is mostly eighth notes, try to figure out a way to make it work as triplets. If the original version was in swung eighth notes, try it in straight eighths and sixteenths, too. Successful improvisors generally use a relatively small amount of material in multiple situations. They make sure their vocabulary is available to them in different keys, in as many rhythmic divisions as possible, and in every practical scale fingering pattern.

Record the variations you produce to to make sure you're executing them in time, and to make sure you're fitting everything together in a sensible way.

Chapter 11: Finding the Phrase Length

Composing and improvising are easier when you know the phrase length each melodic statement must fit. In traditional music forms you identify and play the same phrase length expressed in the chord progression, resolving your part and figuratively taking a breath before a new phrase starts. Having the ability to fit the underlying phrase length at will means your foundation is solid. At times you'll play over these boundaries to create interest, but you should always be able to step back into solid phrasing when needed.

Chord Progression Basics

For our immediate purposes it's not necessary to have a complete knowledge of harmony and theory (though of course it's ultimately recommended) to identify how chords are moving to create a phrase. You can learn to feel it with rudimentary knowledge.

A song is usually only in one **key** at a time, distinguished by a tonal center, the one pitch you could hum that feels like the final note if the song were to stop. We will use the chords in the key of C major for examples, though the same principle applies in every key.

```
C  Dm  Em   F   G  Am  Bdim
I  ii  iii  IV  V  vi  vii
```

The seven chords in the key are grouped into three **families**, each with a psychological effect.

The **tonic** family includes the I, iii, and vi chords. These are the places of rest or resolution. When a progression **starts on** a chord in this family, there is no immediate sense that it has to move to another chord. When a progression **moves to** the tonic family from another family, you will feel a resolution. The sensation is strongest with a move to the I chord, less strong with the vi, and weakest with the iii.

The **dominant** family includes the V and the vii chords. These are the places of tension. You would not usually think of ending a song on a chord of the dominant family. It might feel unfinished. Chords in this family feel like they need to resolve to the tonic. (The word *dominant* is also used to describe the chord type spelled 1 - 3 - 5 - $\flat$7 when starting from its own root. This chord is often introduced on other degrees besides the V to provide tension or harmonic variety.)

The **subdominant** family includes the IV and the ii. This family is not tense but easily moves to either the dominant or tonic family. The subdominant is also a natural place to move **from** the tonic.

A most obvious and typical progression might be tonic-subdominant-dominant-tonic arranged into a four-bar phrase. The progression starts out by establishing the key with a tonic chord, then moves away from it to the subdominant. From there it feels like it may move to either the I or the V. If it moves to the V, we are on a place of tension that wants to resolve back to the I.

```
|C      |F    |G    |C    |
 I       IV    V     I
 T       S     D     T
```

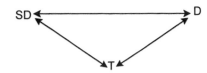

You may move from one chord family to any other (as well as using some chords that may seem to come from an unexplained source) when writing a song, as long as you use tension and resolution to create the sense of a definite phrase length that can be felt by the listener most of the time.

If the listeners can never feel the phrase length, they'll find the music too hard to follow and will bore quickly of trying to make sense of it.

A harmonic phrase could end on either the dominant or subdominant chord families, with only a feeling of partial resolution that implies more is to come. Instead of a simple sentence with a period at the end, think of this type of phrase as part of a compound sentence. A comma shows the reader where a component idea is completed, and must be followed by another clause to finish the sentence.

The feeling of the phrase boundary can be implied by the overall arrangement of chords, or by phrases the listener has already heard in the same song or a similar one. Here are two four-bar phrases, each ending on a different family. You can still hear the phrase length, mostly because they both start on the I, but partly because of tradition. People in Western cultures seem to be programmed to feel four-bar phrases unless pushed into feeling something else.

```
|C          | Am    |G      |F      |
   I           I       V       IV
   T           T       D       S

|C          |G      |C      |G      |
   I           V       I       V
   T           D       T       D
```

When composing lyrics and a melody for the above example, you'd usually put some breathing spaces for the vocalist in measures 4 and 8. A soloist who plays nonstop through all eight measures could exceed the ability of average listeners to follow. You want them to be subconsciously singing along in some way.

Other Phrase Determiners

There always is (or should be) something in the music that happens within a certain number of bars to tell how long the phrases may be. It is usually a repetition, but it could also be a change. If it is not a repeating chord progression, it may be a bass riff, a melodic statement, a drum pattern, or a rhythm part. Phrases are often two, four, or eight bars long, but that's not a rule. It's only a guide, and there are many exceptions. A phrase can be any length that makes sense to the composer. A song might have one four-bar phrase followed by a five-bar phrase. There may also be some measures with a different number of beats from the original time signature.

You should know the length of every phrase you'll be playing over before you start a lead part, and be able to spell out that length for the listener. The main way to do it is to stop playing and take a breath before the next phrase starts. It's nice if your musical idea sounds logical when you stop, but sometimes learning to resolve a phrase smoothly only happens after you force it for a while. First focus on finding where the harmonic phrase pauses (reaches a *cadence*, in classical terms), even if the resolution is not complete.

Everyone in the band should work together at spelling out the phrase length for the listener in their own way. The drummer plays a repeating pattern and may put a fill at the end of a final phrase to set up the next section. The bassist plays a complementary rhythmic pattern to the drummer's and outlines or reflects the chord changes in his pitches. You, as the lead instrument, should also be able to spell out a definite phrase length at will. One sign that you are pulling your weight with your solo is if the listener could still feel the phrase length even if the band were taken out from under you. The first step toward that ability is to **identify** the phrase length played by others when you hear it.

Exercise 4

This time briefly using CD tracks 51, 62, and 73, listen for repetitious elements in the song arrangement to determine the natural phrase length for each. Is it one bar, two, four, eight, or some odd number?

51:

62:

73:

There will be times when some members of the ensemble (including you) play phrases of different lengths from those played by the others, to create a layered effect in the music.

Exercise 5

Listen to three songs, count the bars, and write down the phrase lengths you hear. For most music it won't be very hard. For example, a twelve-bar blues like "Route 66" uses four-bar phrases, as do many rock songs. There are two-bar phrases in the verses to Jimi Hendrix's "Purple Haze" and AC/DC's "Back in Black." Guns & Roses' "Sweet Child O'Mine" uses eight-bar phrases in its verse chord progression. Eight-bar phrases are also common in jazz standards like "All the Things You Are" or "The Girl from Ipanema."

Identifying different phrase lengths on different layers means you hear more possibilities for your own phrasing. In many pop and rock songs, the rhythm instruments play two-bar phrases while the vocal or other melody overlaps them with a four-bar phrase.

Song	Phrase Length(s)
1. Eric Johnson, "Trademark"	4 bars
2.	
3.	
4.	

Assignment

Track 51 is an example of melodic phrasing with spaces for you to copy and absorb. Play the rhythm part with downstroked power chords, then work out the lead melody, which uses a two-bar phrase followed by two one-bar licks, then repeats. When you can play the eight-bar example from memory, write your own phrases that leave a space in the same general areas mine did.

CD Track 51

The first eleven chapters of counting beats and bars, foot-tapping, and practicing scales, sequences, and licks with the metronome were designed to train you to hear the notes you're about to play in your head. Practicing them helps you learn where the downbeat is, and which rhythmic divisions you can play at various tempos. They are also set up to help you feel which bar is the first one in a phrase—when a melody or solo should usually start—and which bar is the last one in a phrase, during which at some point you should be resting or letting a note ring while you get ready to attack the next phrase.

Chapter 12: The Motif

A motif is the smallest musical idea you can identify and repeat. The opening motif of a solo can be as simple as hitting a whole note on the tonic note of the key, right on beat one of the first bar. As long as you can remember it and play it again, it's a motif. It does not need to be unique, striking, or even original. It will become more interesting through repetition, development, and variation, and by being heard over the other instruments. Some of the best opening motifs are just two or three notes played with a clear rhythm that fits the groove. The pitches usually come from a scale or an arpeggio that sets up or spells out the chord in the first measure of the phrase.

Whether composed or improvised on the spot, your solo's first notes have a big role in determining whether it will be successful. You want to come in confidently, making it clear to the listener where the downbeat is, with a solid rhythm feel in your notes. The opposite—stumbling in a few beats late with some stuff that's not in the groove—makes a bad impression and also makes it harder to build the solo into a complete statement. Memorize a few simple motifs, then make sure they're at your fingertips, ready to play in any keys and grooves you expect to encounter. Most motifs that are short can be adapted harmonically to fit any chord, and rhythmically to fit any beat division.

These are example motifs that fit an A minor tonality. Play them in straight eighth notes as written, then listen and imitate as they are adapted to a triplet feel by shuffling the eighth notes, and to a sixteenth-note groove by cutting the note values in half. Some start on the downbeat, and some start earlier with pickups, so be sure to count yourself in correctly.

CD Track 52

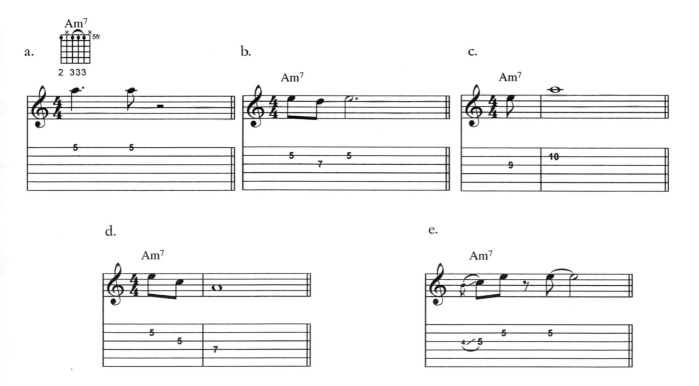

Adapt any new motifs you learn or create to fit as many harmonic situations as possible. Motifs **d** and **e** above contain the minor 3rd degree (in this case, the note C). It must be raised to a major 3rd (C♯) for the motif to be *consonant* with A major or dominant chords. Notice the C♯ in the chord shapes.

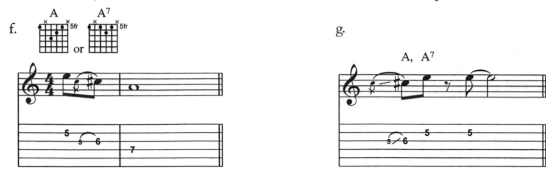

Writing a New Motif

Create your own motif by writing down a rhythm that has one to four eighth-note attacks, and is no more than two beats long. Start within one beat before or after the bar line. Count and play your rhythmic motif until you're sure you know it, then try it out with a couple of A minor scale steps or chord tones (though it's not necessary for all the pitches in a melodic motif to be different). Include the root or fifth; make it simple!

When you find something that sounds reasonably logical, write it down with both rhythm and pitches included. Only add articulations—bending, sliding, etc.—**after** you have defined the rhythm and pitch. Don't get hung up trying to make it spectacular! A motif is just a sentence fragment you will use in the course of telling a bigger story, and at any rate you don't want the climax at the beginning.

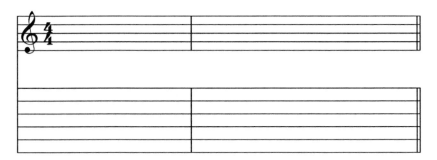

Recording Rhythm Tracks

Many of the exercises from this point on require backing tracks. Recording steady rhythm tracks is a huge part of overall guitar mastery, so don't rely too much on sequencers or jam tracks from other sources. Making your own is the best way. When you start to solo over the track, you'll know the phrasing and accents of the progression or riff, because you played it yourself many times.

You'll start the recorder, turn on the metronome, count beats and bars aloud, and play the rhythm track for the given assignment with the best timing you can muster. Many of the suggested rhythm parts will be sparse, sometimes only using chords in whole notes, so that when you play lead guitar you must create much of the rhythm feel by yourself. If the rhythm track is busy, it can become a crutch. For most soloing practice there should be just enough activity in the rhythm part to define the pulse and the phrase length.

When you play back the recording, you should hear 1) the click—nice and loud, 2) your voice counting beats and bars, and 3) a rhythm guitar part. While listening to the recording you will play a specific lead part that

58

is designed to develop a certain skill. Some may take weeks to master; that's to be expected. As you progress, record the rhythm track again with some or all of the counting taken away, and played at higher tempos. When recording a long chord progression, it can be helpful to just call out "top!" when you get to the end and start over, to help you keep your place while soloing over the playback.

Repetition

With **composed** solos, we can write down or record a motif, memorize it, and practice using it in the places we want it to go. We've been extensively counting beats to get an internal awareness of them as they go by while we play. This makes it possible to identify which beat any **improvised** motif started on so that, if we want, we can repeat it exactly, starting on the same beat in a later measure. This ability, to remember something you've improvised and repeat it on the beat of your choosing, is required to build a logical melody. Improvisation is a similar process to composition, only more streamlined. Learning one supports the other.

Assignment

Record a rhythm track in A minor that's just like the straight eighth-note track for motif examples a-e, but five minutes long, so you can practice repetition of the various motifs. When your rhythm track is in the can, practice each of the motifs from the beginning of the chapter, repeating each one at least three times. Make sure you're counting and starting them on the correct beat every time. Keep your count going between repetitions. If you have overdubbing capacity, record yourself repeating the motifs, then listen to make sure you were right.

When that exercise is comfortable, it's time to step up to alternating between two different motifs, one picking up from beat 4, and the other right on the downbeat.

Over the same rhythm track, alternate between motif **c** and **a** from the list at the beginning of the chapter, starting each motif on its correct beat in the measure. Make sure each motif ends up getting played exactly the same way at least twice. Count aloud during the spaces.

CD Track 53

As soon as you perform it correctly, move on to do the same exercise with two more motifs from the list that start on different beats, say **d** and **e**.

Assignment, Continued

Make sure your fingers and your ears are warmed up a bit before you finally start improvising motifs and repeating them over the track. Play a short motif similar to the others, with just a couple of notes, focusing on the timing. Then play it again in the next measure, exactly the same way—even if you didn't like it. We're building reflexes that will be used when performing live, where you can't reject your own previous choice and start over.

Now improvise a second new motif starting on a different beat, again keeping it simple, so that you can still remember the previous motif, and alternate between the two. If your new motifs were labeled **h** and **i**, you'd be playing this: **h i h i**.

If improvising new motifs seems too hard right now, stop and compose two new ones on paper, making sure each has a different starting beat, then practice until you can apply them on time in alternation. If you have the capacity to record the exercise over the backing track, do so.

Here's the most basic motific repetition I had handy on a real-life recording. The intro melody to "Suite Zero G" uses the same rhythmic motif four times, with different pitches from a variation of the D blues scale. If you play a hardtail, substitute slides for the whammy bar scoops.

CD Track 54

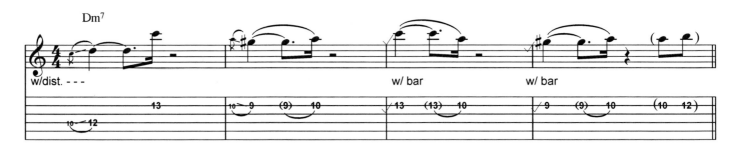

Chapter 13: Building Phrases

Now we'll repeat a motif, but intentionally (not accidentally) move it to a different starting place in the second bar. Just this small variation, a displacement to start a quarter note earlier in this case, can be enough to create interest, because the motif is at a different position against the background. The listener will easily understand and follow the music when there is some repetition balanced with enough variety to keep things moving forward. As you progress you will learn more subtle ways to balance repetition with variation.

If you have a tendency to play solos that wander from one lick to another, you can retrain it by intentionally exaggerating your repetition until it becomes a habit. On the other hand, if you have the tendency to over-repeat yourself so that your solo gets stuck in a rut, you may need to expand your vocabulary of motifs learned from other players, and practice moving them onto other beats, so that your ear opens up to more possibilities.

CD Track 55

In this example, we've got motif **b** from the previous chapter, starting one beat earlier the second time. Because it's a slight variation we might depict it all as **b b2**.

You can think of a motif in your solo as a character in a movie. You wouldn't introduce the protagonist in the first scene and then immediately kill him off, never to be heard of again. In the same way, when the audience hears a motif, they want to know what will happen to it next. If motifs are introduced and then discarded, pretty soon they'll get tired of trying to follow your story. You want to give the audience the feeling that you haven't forgotten the motif you started with. The easiest way to do that: play it again!

End-to-End Connection

This technique can make your soloing more interesting to the listener right away. The last pitch in one improvised figure is followed by a space (a long note or a rest), then repeated at the beginning of the next one. If you stay inside a scale pattern that you're familiar with, it's not too hard. You just have to remind yourself of your intent when you step up to jam.

You could represent end-to-end connected phrasing like this:
Ab bCd dE

The final note of the first motif (**A**) gets a separate label (**b**). The beginning of the next lick starts with the same note and then moves into new territory (**C**), the last note of which (**d**) gets repeated to start the next motif (**E**), and so on.

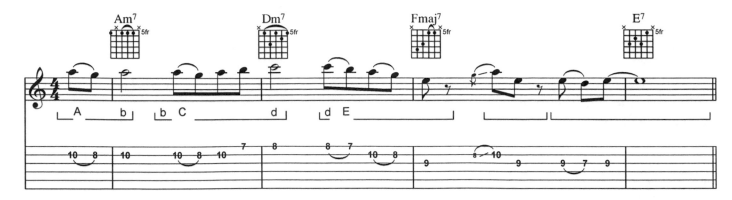

I used mostly single-note connection in the above example, but you can increase the number of notes from the end of one motif used to begin the next one. Here's the same chord phrase, with overlapping connections of two eighth notes, then three eighth notes. The repeated parts are bracketed. Repeating any articulations helps the effect. We've got bending, pull-offs, and some slides.

CD Track 56 cont'd.

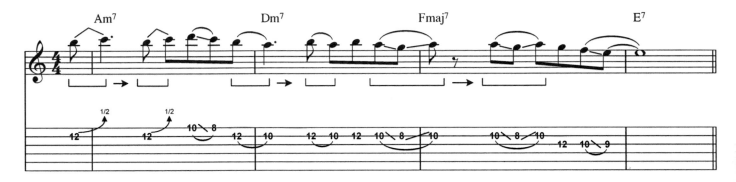

Playing with end-to-end connection in mind can work two ways. You can use the end of one lick as source material to start the next one. Or, if you already know what lick you want to play next, you can foreshadow its first few notes at the end of the current lick, leave a space, then repeat those notes when you play the new lick for real. When part of what they are hearing is familiar, it's easier for the listener to follow you into new territory.

Motific Development

Once an opening motif is established, there are lots of things you can do to develop a melody from it. The one thing you normally should **not** do is forget the motif and start playing something unrelated. On the next page are a few of the many possible developmental processes you can apply to your own ideas.

Assignment

Play the following basic examples, making sure you understand the point of each. Monitor a recording of yourself if you need to be sure you're executing the rhythms. Then write out your own example where you apply each concept to a different motif. Record your development to make sure it works.

a. Repeat part of the original motif but start or finish it differently.

CD Track 57 cont'd.

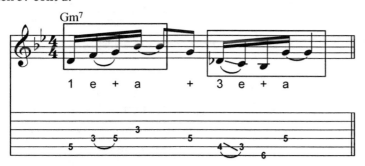

b. Use the same rhythm as the original motif, but with different pitches.

CD Track 57 cont'd.

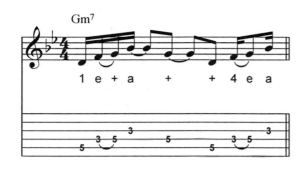

c. Use the same pitches, but with a different rhythm.

d. Repeat the motif or one of its elements at a different rate, e.g. twice per bar.

CD Track 57 cont'd.

e. When all the notes of a motif or theme are increased in duration by the same amount, it's classically known as rhythmic *augmentation*. The opposite is rhythmic *diminution*: decreasing the size of all notes by the same amount, thus shortening the motif by the corresponding length.

CD Track 57 cont'd.

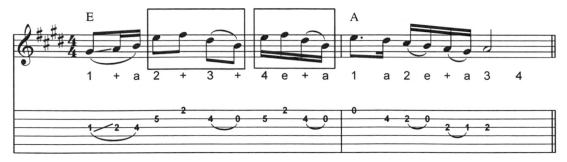

Completing the Phrase

Below is a string of typical developments on a motif from the previous chapter, fit into a four-bar phrase. A displaced repetition (2) of the motif starts a development, adding some variety by heading down a scale. Then the rhythm of motif 1 is used again (3). Another development (4) repeats the notes just introduced but in reverse order and at a faster pace. Each motif is related to the previous one in some way, and may also refer back to an earlier motif.

The analysis may seem rather academic, and it is. Once you learn the principles involved, you don't have to justify everything you play. I just wrote the notes I heard in my head after trying to train myself to phrase with as many connecting threads as possible.

Maybe most importantly, the notes are clear beat divisions played in time, and the melodic idea fits within the confines of the four-bar phrase. When these two apparent restrictions become your habit, you'll paradoxically be able to play with a lot more feeling and creative freedom.

CD Track 58

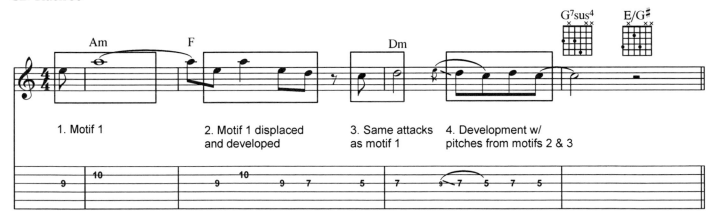

Only if we are intentionally playing a pickup into bar 5 (not shown) do we want to keep playing throughout measure 4. If you overlap the phrase boundary, things may sound fine at first, but soon you could start getting into trouble, making the listener feel like you're searching for something but not finding it. This is especially true when you are improvising. Give your phrases time to breathe and yourself time to think in measure 4.

If you do find yourself playing too long, so that you cross into bar 5, try to stop right there with one note that points out the downbeat for the audience. If you're in a hole, the first thing to do is stop digging. Pause after that single note and use it as a new beginning motif for your next phrase.

You should usually resolve **before** the end of the phrase. Of course there can be exceptions; for example, if this is the final phrase of the song, you might want to play toward that last downbeat. If there is another soloist coming in, you could work out a way for your two parts to overlap in harmony or counterpoint. If you're composing in advance, you may write a section with extra bars to accommodate your idea. Finally, though we're not quite there yet, when building a long solo with increasing intensity the final lick in one phrase may go right up to the next one, either skipping the resolution or only implying it. The word *resolve* doesn't necessarily mean a harmonic resolution to the tonic note here. It's just a pause in the rhythmic structure of your playing.

In some cases a phrase actually requires repetition in order to form a complete idea; the two phrases together are called a *period*, and you would avoid completely resolving your melodic phrase until its end.

If the four-bar progression on the previous page were to repeat as is, I would probably reuse the original motif and its repetition for the next phrase, with some new developments in measures 2 and 3. The idea is to balance familiar ideas with a steady and slow introduction of variety, to keep your audience with you.

A listener probably won't consciously notice how the motifs are related. They'd just feel them as part of something they could follow. I went for the most obvious things I could hear in my head to make a clear example for you. That's how I want you to go about it too. It may only happen sporadically at first, but guide yourself into playing (and writing) what you can hear as making sense.

Assignment

Here's a real-life example of motific development. First learn to play it, then mark and analyze any forms of repetition you can find in it. Then record yourself playing the example to check out your timing.

CD Track 59

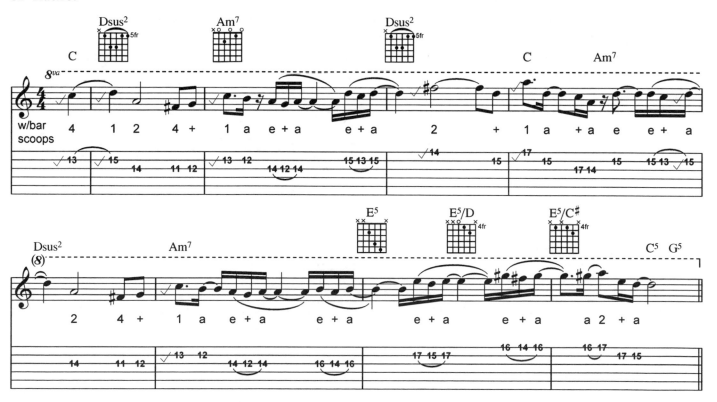

For the next few weeks, approach every opportunity to solo with the intent to only play notes that are related in some way to the ones that came before. You may find yourself feeling better about soloing, because the task is becoming more clearly defined.

- Start with a simple motif.
- Remember it.
- Use it again in some way.
- Fit the phrase length.

Record your playing, check to see if it fits the parameters you've set for yourself, and look for spots where you could have left those extra notes out at the end of a phrase. Don't let little mistakes bother you when you hear them. Just try to fix them next time.

Phrasing Practice with a Partner

Jamming with a practice partner (who can be any kind of instrumentalist—it doesn't have to be another guitar player) can be especially good for learning phrasing if both of you are willing to agree on some organization. A side benefit will be improvement in your ability to play fills to accompany a singer. The more strictly you adhere to the plan, the more useful these exercises will be.

1. Rather than repeating a chord progression indefinitely while the other player solos, take turns soloing for eight, four, or two bars each. Don't allow yourself to overlap the other person's phrase. Finish yours by the downbeat of the last measure, to leave them space to play a pickup phrase if they want. Get right back in the pocket, dropping your volume and playing the chords on the downbeat of the next measure. Be ready to jump back in with one of your prepared motifs, because the turns are short.

2. To practice eartraining at the same time as phrasing, face in opposite directions so you can't see each other. Use a drum machine, rhythm track, or at least a metronome. Agree to a limited range of pitch and rhythm; for example, nothing faster than an eighth-note triplet. You start by playing a simple motific idea that you believe the partner will be able to hear and imitate. He copies it, then plays one for you to imitate. Each soloist first imitates what he has heard, then provides a new phrase for the other. In this example the players trade every four measures.

CD Track 60

Remember the challenge here is not to stump the other guy with a random flurry of notes. Anybody can do that. The goal is to play something so logical and simple that it can't be missed.

3 . Next practice end-to-end connected phrasing with the partner. It's now each player's job to start their turn using only the other's final notes. You'll hear this on jazz recordings. When one soloist finishes, the next will pick up the thread of the last idea.

4. Apply any of the other development techniques in this chapter to material from the other soloist. For example, cop their **opening** motif, and use it to open your phrase, but move into different material to finish it.

Chapter 14: Song Sections

Section types are identified by the function they fill in a song. If you solo over a section later, you should be aware of its original function and only change it for good reason. If the section was quiet and spacious, think twice before you decide to come in with guns blazing. If it was the point of highest energy in the song, keep a high energy level when the section comes up in your solo.

Introductions

An *introduction* establishes the song's rhythm feel and (usually) the key the song will be in, and may contain its own melody or solo. An introduction may be based on (or the same as) a later section of the song. When soloing over an intro, don't get carried away and play your hottest licks, because you'll leave yourself no way to go but down. This sounds obvious on paper, but it's easy to forget. A better idea is to work with bits of an upcoming melody, to suggest to the listener what they'll be hearing later.

We can create an intro from the example in the previous chapter (track 59 on the CD, the "Dust Commander" bridge), by stealing some of its chords and melodic information.

CD Track 61

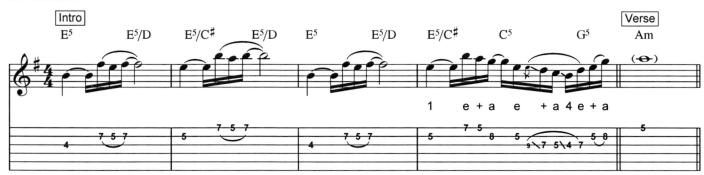

An example of introductory foreshadowing is Steely Dan's "Reelin' in the Years," where part of the progression from the later chorus is used as the introduction. Elliott Randall refers to the chorus vocal melody (with some embellishments like chromatic pull-offs and muted string-scratching) for the first few measures of his intro solo.

Choruses

The word *chorus* has two meanings when discussing song form. In popular music, it's the section that contains the hook, the catchiest part in the song, often with the highest energy level. If you're soloing over a chorus, it can be smart to play (or at least suggest) that hook from the melody in the same spot the vocal did.

In jazz parlance, a *chorus* generally means the part of a chart (or all of it) that is customarily looped for soloing. You might hear a bandleader tell you to "take two choruses," meaning you'd solo through the indicated section twice.

Verses

A verse contains material to support or build up to the chorus. It is generally less energetic and more spacious, to give the chorus greater impact when it arrives. If you're soloing over a verse, you should fit the section length with your phrasing, but you may decide not to quote its original melody, especially if it's already been repeated several times.

Bridges

A *bridge* provides contrast while still relating to the other sections. The contrast can be achieved by changing the rhythm feel, moving through chords at a different rate (a variation in the *harmonic rhythm*), a new key center, or a differently-contoured melody.

More Sections

Another possible section is the *pre-chorus*, which usually follows a verse or bridge and is specifically designed to set up the chorus. More complex compositions may also have an *interlude* (like a bridge, but possibly longer and more of a complete idea unto itself), which can be a composed *solo section* that differs from the rest of the song. Another is the *coda*, which for our purposes is a custom ending or *outro*.

In instrumental music, the traditional terms *verse*, *chorus*, and *bridge* are hard to assign, so section letters may be used instead.

Assignment

Identify sections in one song per day for the next week. Write down the complete order of sections and the number of bars in each section, like this.

The Beatles, "Taxman"

Intro	2 bars
Verse	8
Chorus	5
Verse	8
Chorus	5
Bridge	9
Solo Verse	8
Chorus	5
Verse	8
Chorus	5
Verse	8
Chorus	7
Solo Verse	Fade

Layering Phrases in a Section

A section of any type may be comprised of repeating short harmonic phrases or bass riffs, usually one, two, or four measures long. You can think of these phrases as a foundation of concrete blocks. Melodies and solos can layer longer beams on top of these blocks. This diagram represents the general idea.

If you have a one- or two-measure repeating chord progression or bass riff to play over, concentrate on four-bar phrasing in the lead part. In the following excerpt from "Birds of Prey," there is a one-bar bass riff (doubled with guitar) adapted to follow a two-bar chord progression. Over this foundation is a four-bar melody using the E Dorian mode. The example contains three layers of phrase length: the bass riff (one bar), the harmony (two bars), and the melody (four bars).

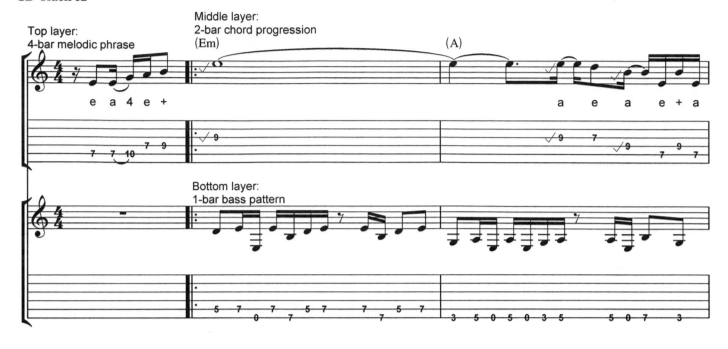

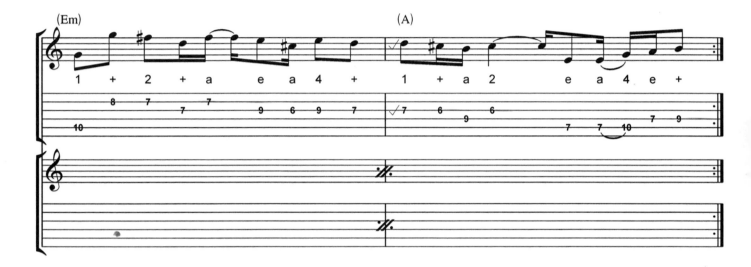

A good example of layering is Jeff Beck's classic "Freeway Jam," (written by Max Middleton). At 1:29 in the recording you'll hear the two-bar bass pattern switch to a catchy one-bar line. Four bars later (at 1:36), the main eight-bar guitar melody starts. Having the new bass part start four bars early in this case was an effective idea, keeping the listener from having to follow two compositional changes at once. Max keeps up his improvisational keyboard comping to counter the stricter parts.

> An *arrangement* results from the process of *arranging*: creating parts for instruments and determining a section order to flesh out a basic compositional idea. As with good phrasing of a single part, a good arrangement provides contrasts of space and density, for example by having some instruments remain silent at times.

A layered arrangement can be composed from the bottom up or from the top down, depending on which part you come up with first. If you already have a long melodic line or chord progression and you want to create a bass part to fit under it, try using a one- or two-bar pattern for contrast.

The opposite idea, layering short but complete phrases on top of longer ones, is another valid option. Here are 2-bar phrases on top of the three 4-bar phrases created by the chord progression of a basic 12-bar blues.

CD Track 63

Outline Long Phrases

In most song forms it's a good idea to outline each sectional phrase created by the chords when you want your playing to be as melodic as possible. A song may demand a bit more effort from the listener to understand when it has long phrases in its chord progression, or phrases of varying lengths. In those cases, you want to help them feel the main phrase downbeats, though your solo may still be comprised of multiple short motifs.

Blues Forms

In a **twelve-bar blues** there are three phrases of four bars each. To support the phrases, nail the downbeats on measures 1, 5, and 9 with a tone you're sure will work on the I, IV, and V chords, respectively. I'm using short pickup phrases into those tones here. Put a bit of breathing space in measures 4, 8, and 12. Other than taking care of these requirements now and then, just play from the heart, not your head.

CD Track 64

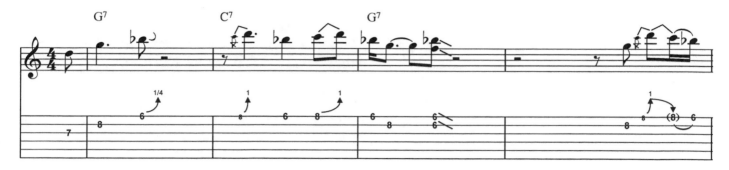

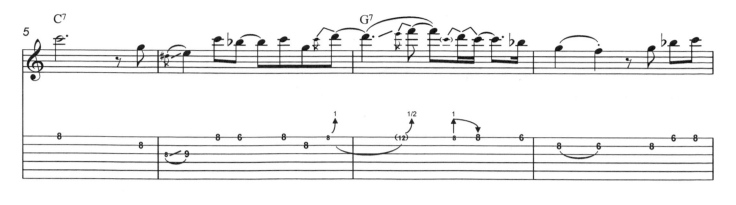

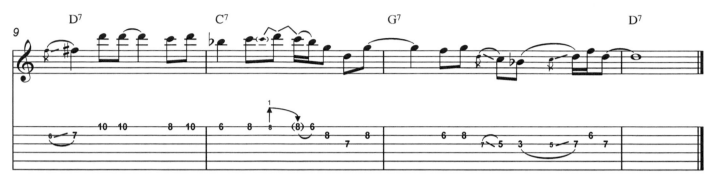

In an **eight-bar blues,** there are usually two main four-bar phrases. You can divide that up into smaller two-bar pieces in your mind. For me it feels good to have resolutions in bar 4, 3/4 of the way through the first phrase, and in bar 7, 3/4 of the way through the entire progression. I've marked these two places in the example, and as you can see, that point in measure 7 is often followed by a turnaround lick.

CD Track 64 cont'd.

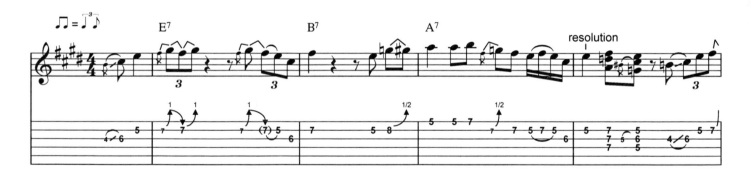

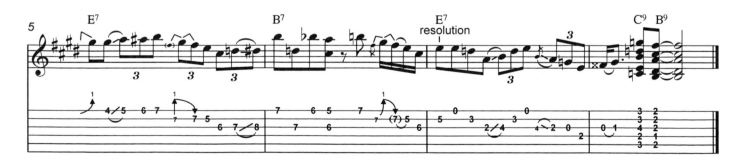

Standards

The most common song form in the book is the 32-bar AABA standard, with four eight-bar phrases. The B section (a bridge) should have a contrasting melodic structure to the A sections. There are already thousands of examples of solos over 32-bar tunes and similar variations out there, and delving into them here would take this book into territory some students may not be ready for, because along with the increased phrase lengths in the jazz style come more-advanced harmonic concepts.

For those who are ready, however, one of the best things you can do for your phrasing abilities is get the *Real Book* (which is really a *fake book*) and learn standards like "Autumn Leaves," "April in Paris," and "As Time Goes By" (and those are just some of the A's). Learn and analyze the chords and the melodies, and transcribe or read solos, starting with swing-era giants like Louis Armstrong and Charlie Christian, and moving into the bebop era with Charlie Parker, Dizzy Gillespie, etc.

Odd Numbers of Bars

Identify progressions of irregular length. Because they're already odd, outlining any existing phrasing should be enough complexity. You can often take your phrasing cues from the vocal melody or a signature line if the section appeared before. In this example, the chords point to the Em chord, a tonic family member in the key of G, as a resolution point. The 5th measure may have been there originally to accommodate a lyric pickup into the next downbeat. The two measures of Gmaj7 may be the beginning of a new section, or they may complete a twelve-bar section (5 + 5 + 2). Irregularly-numbered phrases within familiar forms are a way to make a song more interesting yet still coherent.

CD Track 65

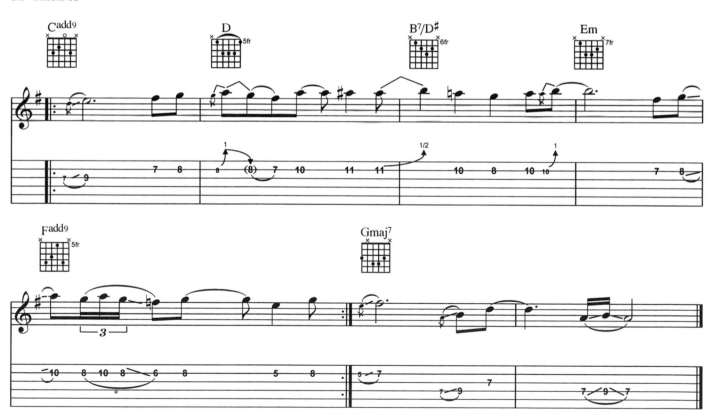

One-Chord Vamps

A *vamp* is any figure or chord progression that is repeated for a long time while something else happens. The "something else" could be a dance contest, a voiceover, or just a solo section on one chord. Sixteen-bar or longer vamps occur in many styles of music, especially in live situations. These sections are more rewarding for listeners when you help them keep their place with your phrasing chops. As with the previous blues examples, accent the first downbeat of the recurring phrase (measure 5, 9, 13, etc.), and place resolutions 3/4 of the way through the phrases (measure 4 and 8, or measure 7 if it feels like an eight-bar phrase).

Open Jams

A possible problem in a open-jam situation is a lack of concerted phrasing by the band. There may be a one-chord vamp with no tension and resolution happening at any particular time. Most drummers will try to play longer even-numbered patterns, so listen for a fill or even just an open hi-hat every four or eight bars. Start putting your breathing space there and phrasing with him or her. Generally speaking you'll have the most luck trying to find an existing phrase and emphasizing it so that other jammers may hear it the same way and work with it.

When you're the first person to set up a new groove, you can try to introduce a four- or eight-bar phrase. Usually the rhythm section will hop right on any structure. Once you've got a phrase length set by your riff, try not to let it drift; hang with it for an even number of times and try for a resolution that implies an even larger section.

If you're in the middle of a jam and you're sure no one is playing a phrase longer than one measure (remember that drummers almost always have a longer phrase length in mind), you can try to introduce one. If your suggestion is too complex or polyrhythmic, most good drummers and bassists will play it safe and not try to follow it unless it's rehearsed. Just repeat a simple two- or four-bar rhythm with a clear starting beat, staying in the same time signature as everyone else.

Chapter 15: Form and Pacing

As within phrases and sections, the principles of repetition, variation, development, and connected phrasing can apply between one section and a later one, in the larger time frame of the entire form.

At this level we're concerned with how many sections our solo must fit into and fill. We also want to consider higher functions, like building to a climax, or bringing the song back down, setting up sections that follow.

> There is a rhythmic sense of place at every level: in the measure, in the phrase, in the section, in the form of the song, and even beyond if you want to consider it: the order of songs in a set, the sets in a show, and so on.

Short and Concise

Very often you have to get in, say what you have to say in four or eight bars, and smoothly exit. Have one simple motif ready; a snippet of the song's melody is a good source. Relax, count off and jump in with it, then develop it further if there is time, but don't step on the next section, especially if it is a vocal part. You'll keep getting work if your solos hand the song over to the singer on a silver platter, so that he or she barely has to think about how to come in. Make eye contact with them just before you finish. Consider ending your solo on their starting pitch (and/or yours, if you'll be singing a harmony), then stepping aside for an entire measure before the vocals begin.

Building Up

When you have multiple sections to solo over, you'll usually want to pace things so that you build up energy as you go along. You don't want to peak too early and run out of gas before the end. To make it work, you have to start at a lower energy level than your anticipated climax will be. Start low and slow, and spread your development out over the time you have. Mick Taylor's solo at the end of "Can't You Hear Me Knockin'" is a good basic example to learn and copy. Gradually increase the frequency of licks, the density of notes, and complexity of ideas, and possibly move higher in pitch as you go.

Your audience's state of mind is different from yours. Especially if you are improvising, you may be thinking hard to decide what you want to play. The audience is just enjoying the music. While you are focusing on your part and all the things that may lie ahead, they are hearing a mixture of all the instruments in the present moment only, with an occasional expectation about what will happen in the next few beats. They may be paying attention to you only part of the time, so you should usually repeat or stretch out a musical idea for longer than you might expect. The listeners will be just starting to notice that you're repeating or developing an idea and beginning to wonder where it will go, even though **you** think you have already played it out and should be moving on to something else.

Tell the audience what you are going to say. Say it. Then tell them what you said. Then you can move on and repeat the process, gradually developing the ideas into higher complexity until you reach the climax point, usually about half to two-thirds of the way through the solo.

Breaking the Mold

If you've established a pattern where the audience has been able to easily follow you and predict some of what you will play, that means you now have them in your pocket. At this point they're mentally ready for new material, so this is where you can play a lick that is unrelated to the previous ones. A jazz musician might play outside the harmony. But besides the choice of notes, just about anything can work once when you are going for sheer variety or surprise. You can suddenly become quiet when you'd expect it to be loud. You can change your tone, or let your guitar feed back on a long note when they're expecting a fast lick.

If you've been playing complicated ideas, you could switch to a simple one. Some players like to phrase melodically within a seven-note scale for the first part of a solo, then switch over to raunchier pentatonic or blues licks when it's time to take the party up a notch. Here's a medium-length (16 bars) example from "Wrecked on the Sirens' Rocks." The blues-scale licks in the last line have a greater impact there than if the solo had opened with them. The 8-bar bass riff rhythm figure is included beneath.

CD Track 66

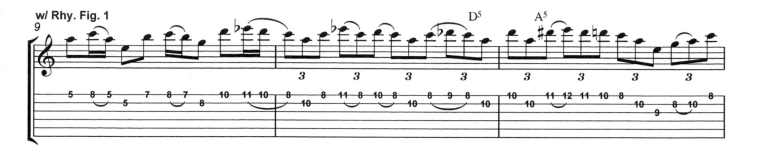

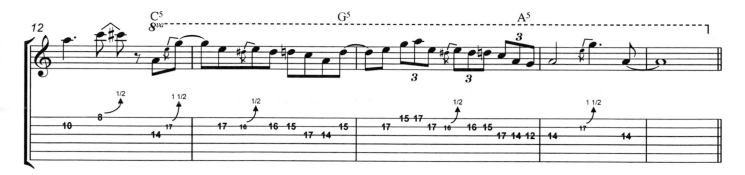

You can hear a similar switchover in Jeff Beck's " 'Cause We've Ended As Lovers," (written by Stevie Wonder) at 3:17, where he caps off an ascending buildup with a familiar rock lick, making it sound fresh again.

Sustain the Intensity

If you've reached a climax point about half to 2/3rds of the way into a long solo, you still have time to keep the fire burning. At maximum intensity, licks may run together without little to no space between phrases, or they may overlap the phrase or section boundary, but don't overdo it or you'll lose the audience. You should still be aware of the place where a resolution would normally go, even when there is no apparent breathing space. Don't throw caution to the wind and start riffing at random. Keep your ideas connected to each other, and keep track of your position in the section.

The Close

Whatever time frame we've been working with throughout this book, I've suggested making a practice of stopping the flow of notes about 3/4 of the way through it. This gives the listener and you time to absorb the previous phrase and prepare for a new one. The same principle often applies to entire solos, but now instead of stopping we have time to make a more involved closing statement. The main objective is to tell the listener that your solo is ending, and to appropriately lead into the next section.

Bring It Down? Or Go Out with a Bang?

Often it's musically appropriate to taper off in your last few phrases, using ideas that are less complex than previous ones, returning to a lower register and volume before you finish your solo. Other times you can go out with some fireworks as you tell the listener that there's nothing left to say. One way to choose is based on what is coming up next.

If your solo is followed by a lower-energy verse or bridge or any melodic section in an instrumental that is less dense than your solo (and they usually will be), tapering off during the end of your solo will help keep that next section from feeling anticlimactic. The same usually applies if there is to be another soloist following you. Bring it down and make a smooth handoff, so that the next player has room to start off low and build up again.

On the other hand, if your solo will be followed by a high-energy chorus, or you are trading short solos with another instrument near the end of a song, you may be able to fan the flames right through your last phrase. There is no definite rule about which way is right at a given time. Be sensitive to the situation and aware of what will come next, and think of contributing rather than showing off. What's most musical? Either way, you should help the listener to predict in advance that your solo is ending, with no awkward surprises.

Open Solos

Your solo may be *open* in that there is no one telling you how many times to play through a given progression. The band will vamp on that progression until you give them an obvious (musical, or even better, visual) cue to move into the next section. In this case you should immediately become your own producer and consciously decide in advance how many choruses you'll take. It's one of the biggest advantages you can give yourself for many reasons. The most obvious is that you know when to hit your peak, and when to taper off.

Plan for fewer choruses rather than more. You can always add an extra one when you reach the end, but it's impossible to get out of the "one too many" once you're into it. There's more music after you in the song, possibly with more soloists who are waiting to play, and you don't want to wear out the crowd. If you're playing more solos tonight, you don't want to exhaust your vocabulary. Finally, planning to take only two choruses instead of three or four will remind you to stick with one idea per section and develop it, because you don't have all night to blow licks until you stumble across something that feels fresh and inspiring to you. Of course, if at the tail end of the second chorus you feel like it would sound more balanced and complete to add another one, go ahead and take it. That's why the solo is open.

Exercise 6

Learn, play, and analyze this solo from "Healer," marking any motifs, repetitions, and developments with alphabetical labels to help you keep track of what is happening. If there is a buildup to a climax, mark it, and mark any tapering-off phrases.

CD Track 67

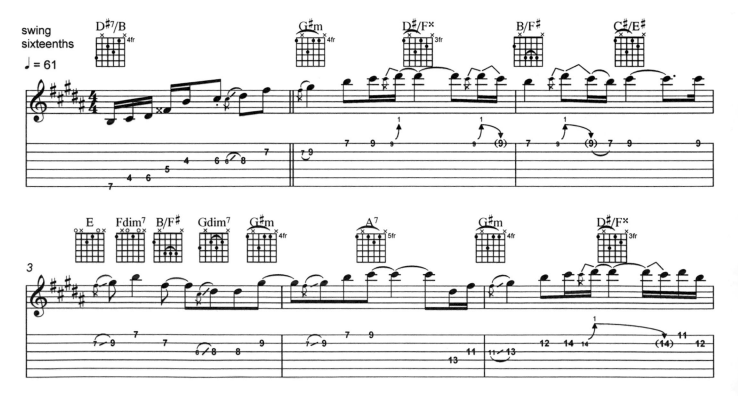

Assignment

Get some staff paper, then transcribe, learn, and memorize a well-structured solo by an established musician. Transcribe from the recording yourself, taking as long as necessary to get as close as you can to the original. If it's your first transcription, don't expect perfection or speed. The first one can take weeks or months, and it's likely to be full of mistakes you'll notice if you check it out a year later.

Figure out everything, starting with the bass notes, then the chords, any extra rhythm parts, and the basic drumset pattern, before tackling the solo. Analyze and mark your transcription. Where are phrases completed in the solo? Do they relate to the phrasing of the other instruments? What are the scales being used? Are any chord tones being targeted by the player? Where are the breathing spaces?

If you've never made a transcription and are wondering which solos would be easy to transcribe and play but still informative from a phrasing standpoint, here are a few suggestions. I chose these because they should be easy to find, and everyone is likely to be familiar with at least one of them.

The Allman Brothers, "Ramblin' Man" – Classic Rock
Albert King, "Crosscut Saw" – Blues
Pure Prairie League, "Amy" – Country
Miles Davis, "All Blues" – Jazz
Red Hot Chili Peppers, "Californication" – Modern Rock

Regular transcribing is one way to steadily improve as a player, especially if you go about it intelligently. Don't just memorize licks and parrot them at random. Think about why they sounded right at the time they were played. While the experience is fresh in your mind, compose your own example that uses what you've learned.

Chapter 16: Additive Rhythms

We started playing scales in groups of five in Chapter 10. The ear identifies the first note of each group as a starting point, creating syncopated accents that contrast with the normal ones in the time signature. Grouping notes at the beat division level can spur creation of new melodies, chord changes, rhythmic accents, bass riffs, and solo phrases.

Notes in measures or phrases may be grouped in any way. Some contrast with the pulse of the original meter. For example, a bar of eight eighth notes can be grouped like this: 123 123 12. The accents can be created with melodic movement, chord attacks, *dynamics* (changes in volume), or any other method you might think of as long as the beginning of each group has the same differentiating quality.

CD Track 68

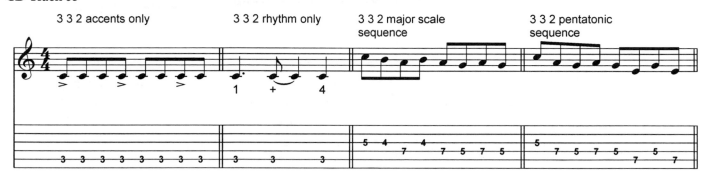

When playing these examples, it's best to keep the foot tapping in the same old quarter notes as always. Be careful not to start tapping your foot along with the syncopated rhythm. Irregular foot-tapping will only become necessary when playing odd time signatures. These examples are still in 4/4 time.

Keeping only the accented notes in the final example above creates a simple but effective Latin-influenced bass figure. To hear it in action, dig up Eddie Cochran's "Twenty Flight Rock" and check out the verses.

CD Track 68 cont'd.

While we're near the subject, some Latin music is organized around a recurring rhythmic figure called a *3:2 clave* (Spanish for *key*). The 3:2 part of the name comes not from the groupings but just from the fact that there are three attacks in the first measure and two in the second. A 2:3 clave has the same measures in reverse order. Below are just four of many variations. *Son* is a Cuban music style; *bossa nova* is Brazilian.

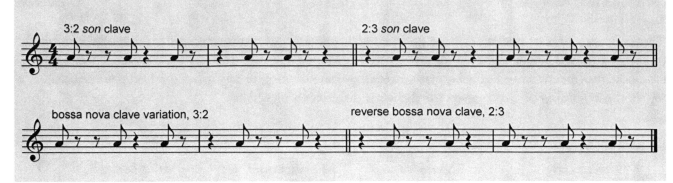

A commonly-used additive rhythm groups two measures of eighth notes (or one of sixteenths) like this: 3+3+3+3+2+2 (123 123 123 123 12 12), giving us signature parts in "Barracuda" (first heard in a high guitar line at 1:12), "Here Comes the Sun" (after each chorus), "I Shot the Sheriff" (after each verse), and many others.

Assignment

Complete this exercise in 10 minutes or less. Don't think too much. Write.

1. First write a series of 2s, 3s, and/or 4s that add up to 16.
   Sample: 3 2 3 2 3 3

   Yours:

2. Apply the scheme to an A minor pentatonic scale to start an eighth-note-based riff. You can use eighth notes, longer notes including dotted quarter notes and any necessary ties, and/or rests, as long as you can feel the additive rhythm accents you planned. Break up the scalar movement with melodic jumps or repeated pitches.

When the above is complete, you should have the first two measures filled. Here's mine:

CD Track 69

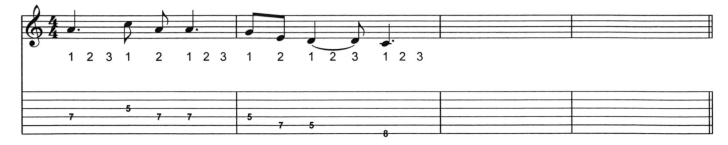

Yours:

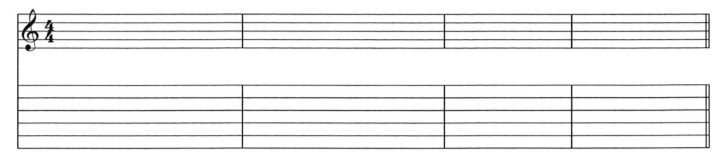

3. Now skip over and put a whole note on the root (A) or 5th (E) in measure 4.

4. Finally, use your ear to decide what might work in measure 3. Add articulations where they make sense to you. Don't agonize over making it perfect; just knock out a riff that sounds ok. If you want to keep working, write another one with a pickup bar.

Sample riff:

CD Track 69 cont'd.

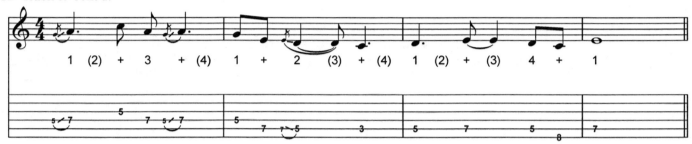

Building Licks from Groupings

Besides these band figures, additive rhythms make useful solo devices that are good for building tension when repeated several times in a row. The listener feels the lick's pattern contrasting with the pulse pattern, and wonders when and how they will come back together. You fulfill their expectations when you finish the lick and resume the original pattern of accents. It's up to you to decide how long to ride one of these ideas.

A 2 + 4 structure is the basis for repetitive soloing figures like this one used by Jimmy Page, Ronnie Montrose, and many others from the classic rock era. The lick is one and a half beats long when played in sixteenth notes, so you can play it four times and come out on beat 3 of measure 2. When played in triplets it's exactly two beats long, so you can start it on beat 1 or 3 and it will always be easy to finish gracefully.

CD Track 70

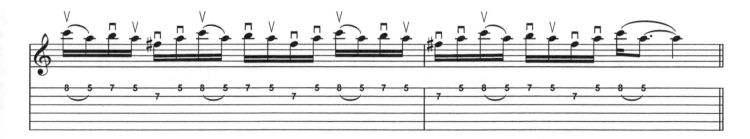

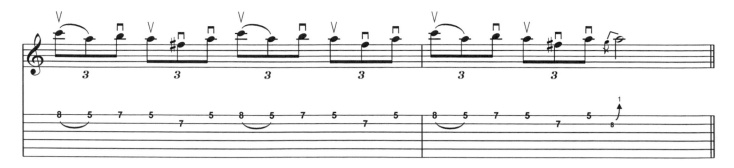

Each player sounds a little different on it, with most using legato technique for the 2nd and/or 4th note. I've notated one way I like to play it that is percussive and driving. Notice how it sounds when picked differently and decide which works best for you.

A variation of the above lick is used to build up energy in the "Birds of Prey" solo. It feels like this to me: 3 + 2 + 3 + 2 + 3 + 3, though the final 3s are created by pick accents only. You may hear 2 + 2 + 2 at the end. The licks use a combination of the E blues scale and the E Dorian mode, moving higher with each iteration. This excerpt starts in bar 3 of an eight-bar phrase.

CD Track 71

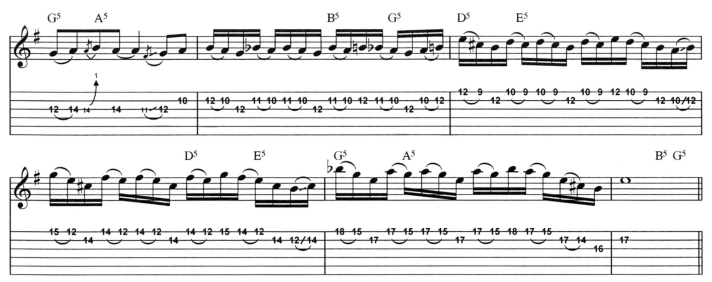

Assignment

Now I'd like you to work along with me and write a one-bar triplet rock lick with syncopation created by additive rhythm. Write any series of 2s, 3s, and/or 4s that adds up to 12. Mine will be 2 + 3 + 3 + 4. Yours should be a little different. If it is all 3s there will be no syncopation.

Mine: 2 3 3 4

Yours:

Apply your groupings to triplets, using notes from the A Dorian mode (A B C D E F# G). Accent the first note of each group so you can hear where each one starts. Try the pitches in various positions until you find the one that is easiest to play and sounds best. Mine worked out well in 7th position.

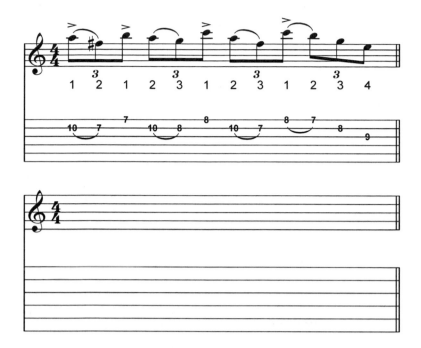

Practice playing your new lick three times in a row, then end it in measure 4. I'd end mine with a whole note on A in measure 4, but you might add or subtract a group at the end to make it more interesting, and finish on a different tone.

Use Additive Rhythms to Write Syncopated Melodies and Lines

Here we'll start with a simple theme based on an additive rhythm, and then develop it into a more complex line for when the theme returns later in the song. The following two excerpts are from "Suite Zero G." First learn the chorus chords, then the melody. It's pretty basic, with the 3 + 3 + 2 pattern implied by long notes in measures 1-3 and 5-7.

CD Track 73

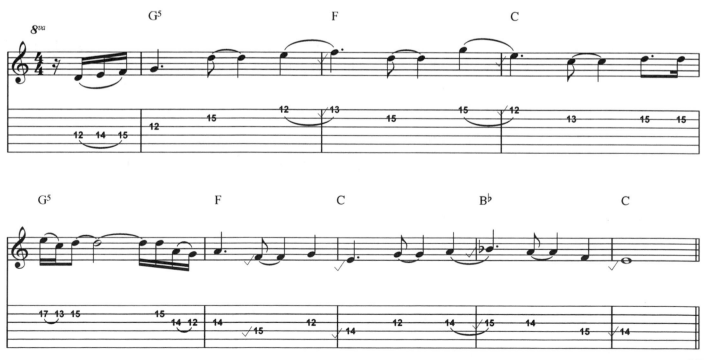

When the part is recapped later, the basic melody is fleshed out with arpeggios and scalar connections to create a rolling line with syncopated rhythmic patterns built in. This kind of line should be worked out on paper and practiced until it's smooth. Let's analyze a few bars at a time.

Bits of a 3 + 3 + 2 grouping pattern in 16th notes were woven in with the existing melodic thread wherever they fit. You can start a pattern at whichever beat suits your purpose, as in these first three measures, where it appears on beat 3 of bar 1. In this case, we're alternating the rhythmically-shaped arpeggios (chords spelled one note at a time) with scalar connections to the next chord.

For the string-skipping arpeggios, try hybrid picking (using the pick and middle finger), or outside picking (upstrokes on the high strings, downstrokes on the low strings), combined with legato technique where possible.

CD Track 73 cont'd.

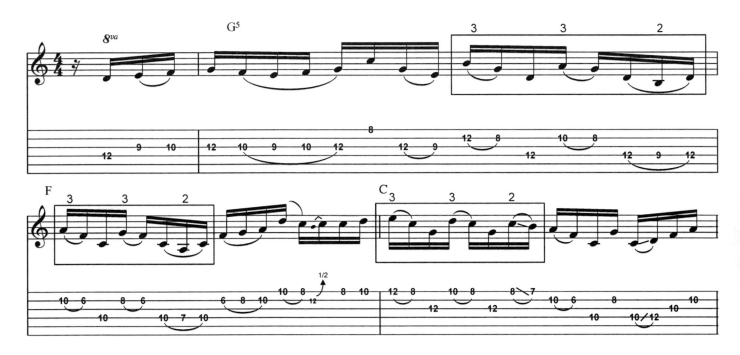

In measure 4 a tension-building sequence moves three steps up the C major scale: 1276 2317 342 (the last group is incomplete). The sequence goes up a step, down a 3rd, then down a step.

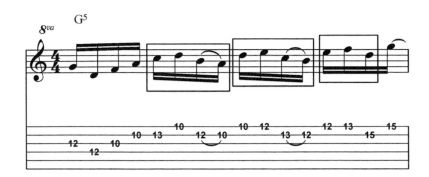

The F chord in measure 5 uses G and E (the 9th and 7th) as target tones.

Measure 6 introduces a triplet motif on beat 3. The motif is repeated on a higher pitch in measure 7, first on the downbeat, then displaced to the "and" of 2. Chord tones are targeted on the C, but the first tone on the B-flat chord is its sharp eleventh, E. The B-flat major triad only requires that the B in the scale be dropped to B-flat. We're still in the G Mixolydian tonality here (or C major—they share the same notes; the only difference is whether you hear G or C as the tonic).

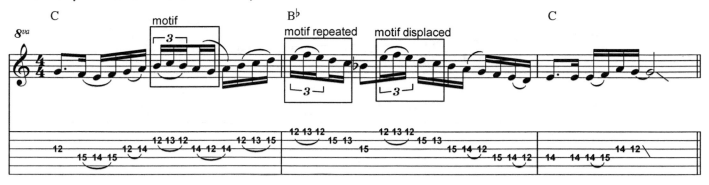

Such complex combinations of rhythmic and phrasing ideas might be a bit much at the beginning of a tune. When it does become appropriate, however, the more accent patterns, motifs, and sequences you can work into a section at once (and still have it all make sense), the more potential it has to appeal to the listener, because while it is all repetitive pattern-oriented content, it's broken up and interwoven in an interesting way.

With repeating additive rhythms as an underpinning, you can create a lot of new musical structures, from simple to complicated, over a 4/4 groove. The pattern may be obvious, with every band member powering out all the groupings, or subtle, with just a hint of it in a few bars of your solo that goes away before it has a chance to be fully recognized.

Assignment

Here is another rock lick, from "Devil's House Party." This time I would like you to mark the groups and write out the additive rhythm they come from.

CD Track 74

Chapter 17: Pedal Tones

Apedal tone embedded in a line of notes is yet another way to impose continuity and repetition for melodic development. In this chapter we'll play a scale with a pedal tone included, learn some typical pedal-tone based licks, and finally use pedal tones in a longer line along with some syncopated accents.

In its original meaning a pedal tone was a bass note held under moving chords using a church organ foot pedal. Besides a sustained drone, the term *pedal tone* (also pedal *point*) can refer to any recurring note (usually the tonic or fifth of the key center) that is interspersed with another part that moves. The pedal tone may be below, above, or in the middle of a scalar passage. Here's a Pattern-3 E major exercise with a tonic pedal that stays on the top as the scale descends, then keeps a tonic pedal on the bottom as the scale ascends.

CD Track 75

Any pattern you practice with a major scale should also be applied to its modes. Here's the B Mixolydian mode (equivalent to E major Pattern 3) in 8th position. Now the likely pedal tones are B and F♯.

CD Track 75 cont'd.

Ostinato vs. Pedal Figure

An *ostinato* is any pattern that is repeated continuously, with little to no change. Ostinati may be bass lines, rhythm parts, and in some cases even may comprise an entire melody. By traditional definition an ostinato hammers away nonstop (the word is Italian for *obstinate*), but we can also repeatedly inject a pattern of notes within other movement, just as we do with pedal tones. For clarity's sake, let's call this a *pedal figure*.

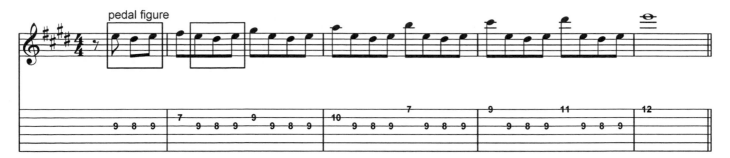

A Syncopated Pedal-Tone Line

The E major scale and B Mixolydian mode used in the previous examples are applied using some sliding and multiple pedal points in an excerpt from "Delta Queen." Ties to beat 3 follow the rhythm section's syncopation at the sixteenth-note level

CD Track 77

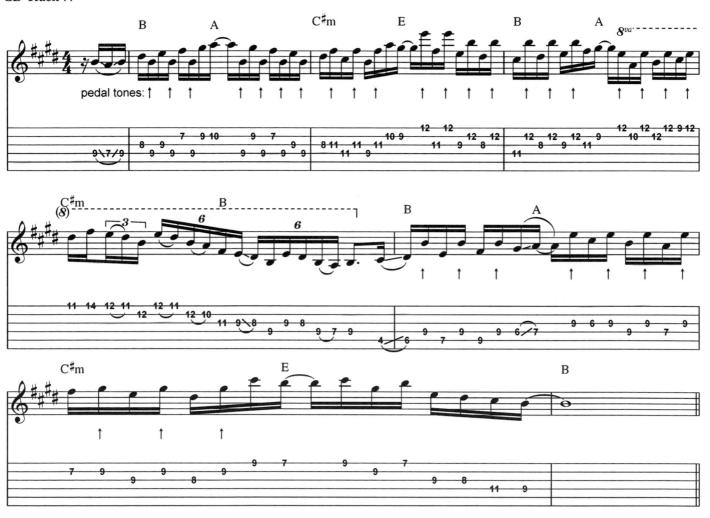

Pedal-Based Blues Licks

With more liberal interpretation, pedal tones and figures become the motific glue in bluesy piano-style phrases.

CD Track 78

Pedal Tone Sequences

A pedal can be used as the background or filler for a sequencing idea. The listener's attention is directed toward the part that is moving. Using an open string for the pedal tone is an easy way to start. Here are groups of two scale steps alternating with the open E, to form groups of three in sixteenth notes.

CD Track 78 cont'd.

Here's a pedal-tone riff that crosses the bar line with the additive rhythm structure 322 322 322 3. Add emphasis to the notes with the accent marks. Doubling the line with the bass player and having the drummer reinforce the first note of each group would create an interesting figure that might conclude a section.

CD Track 78 cont'd.

Assignment

Make your own pedal point line for this progression using straight eighth or sixteenth notes. E natural minor is the suggested scale. Your pedal tone should be E or B. If you come up with one you like, transpose and practice it over the same progression in other keys; it's very common.

Sample:

CD Track 78 cont'd.

Yours:

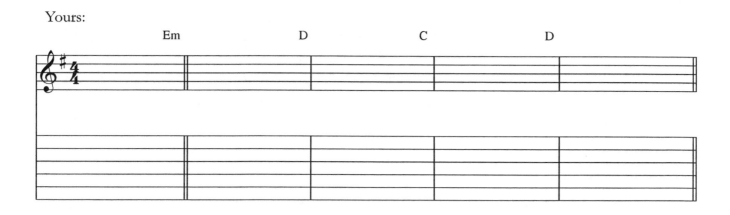

Chapter 18: Odd Meters

Odd meters have note groupings of different sizes within one measure. The basis for these groupings is in meters we already know. We mentally group notes into twos and threes (and sometimes fours, for convenience) to define accent patterns. The first note of each group is accented.

Groups of Two

The usual pattern of quarter note accents in unsyncopated 4/4 time is two groups of two.

$$\underline{1\ \ 2}\ \ \underline{3\ \ 4}$$
$$(\underline{1\ \ 2}\ \ \underline{1\ \ 2})$$

When we look at the eighth notes, there are four groups of two, and we tap the foot only on the first of each.

$$\underline{1\ +}\ \ \underline{2\ +}\ \ \underline{3\ +}\ \ \underline{4\ +}$$
$$(\underline{1\ \ 2}\ \ \underline{1\ \ 2}\ \ \underline{1\ \ 2}\ \ \underline{1\ \ 2})$$

Groups of Three

In 3/4 time, the first quarter note is accented.

$$\underline{1\ \ 2\ \ 3}$$

The eighth notes in unsyncopated 3/4 time occur as three groups of two.

$$\underline{1\ +}\ \ \underline{2\ +}\ \ \underline{3\ +}$$
$$(\underline{1\ \ 2}\ \ \underline{1\ \ 2}\ \ \underline{1\ \ 2})$$

At high tempos, 3/4 time may be tapped "in one," making it a compound single meter. Now the beat is a dotted half note. Tap the foot once per measure.

$$\underline{1(2\ \ 3)}$$

An example song for taking 3/4 in one is "Carol of the Bells."

In a compound meter like 12/8, eighth notes are grouped in threes. Again, the first note of each group is where the foot naturally taps.

$$\underline{1\ +\ a}\ \underline{2\ +\ a}\ \underline{3\ +\ a}\ \underline{4\ +\ a}$$
$$(\underline{1\ \ 2\ \ 3}\ \ \underline{1\ \ 2\ \ 3}\ \ \underline{1\ \ 2\ \ 3}\ \ \underline{1\ \ 2\ \ 3})$$

An odd meter, for our purposes, is any meter with at least one group of three and one group of two, whether at the quarter-note or the eighth-note level or smaller. The groups may be in any order. We'll start with the quarter-note level.

Odd Quarter-Note Meters
Five-Four

Some 5/4 songs are "Take Five" (Paul Desmond), "Living in the Past" (Jethro Tull), "English Roundabout" (XTC), and "Morning Bell" (Radiohead, *Kid A*). 5/4 usually has accents on beats 1 and 4,

$$\underline{1\ \ 2\ \ 3}\ \ \underline{4\ \ 5}$$
$$(\underline{1\ \ 2\ \ 3}\ \ \underline{1\ \ 2})$$

though it could have accents on 1 and 3, in which case you'd reverse the grouping order (1 2 1 2 3).

The first thing to remember about playing in 5/4 is that you **count off** in 5/4 before you start. Tap the foot in quarter notes, and count aloud while strumming the chord pattern below. It takes time to get used to a new meter. When it's solid, play the single note part while counting. First we're making sure you can copy the existing accent pattern, nailing beat 1 and beat 4.

CD Track 79

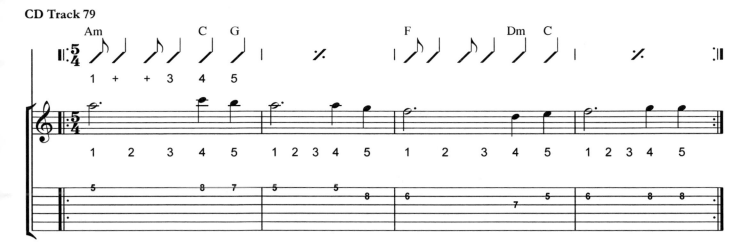

When the above is comfortable, we keep the main accent pattern but add pickups, dotted notes, and ties to create some syncopation, along with a few articulations for character. Keep the foot taps going.

CD Track 79 cont'd.

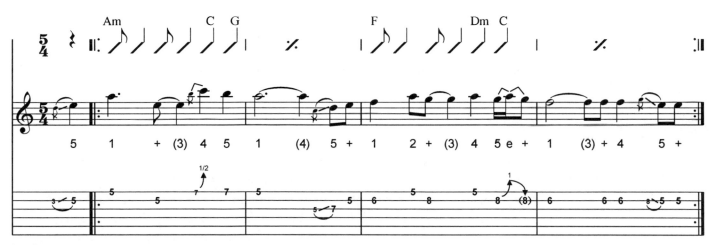

Assignment

When you can play the above example with steady time (which may take a while; be patient), record a 5/4 progression for five minutes, then practice adapting your reflexes to play your existing two- and three-note motifs over it. Don't let the downbeat get away from you. Avoid forcing 4/4 phrasing onto the meter; it'll make you sound like you're lost. A discerning listener will know if it's right, so step back and play less until you really feel the time.

All the principles we learned for soloing in 4/4 time also apply to any meter: keep track of the downbeat and show it to the listener, respect the phrase length, repeat and develop motifs, and so on. New phrasing reflexes have to develop, so learning to improvise in odd meters can feel like starting over as a beginner. Odd meters appear in all styles of music more than you might expect, so it's important to have a basic understanding of them.

It can be useful to think of 5/4 as alternating bars of 3 and 2. The sound is the same; only your count changes. Sometimes a composer will help you by specifying the note grouping with an additive time signature.

Seven-Four

Let's try another odd quarter note meter, this time a rock riff in 7/4. This is the intro to "Girth-Hankering Days." The natural accents are on 1, 3, and 5, but the riff contains some syncopation. It's ok to think of 7/4 as alternating bars of 4 and 3, or any other combination that adds up to the same time. You won't have the two-syllable word "seven" tripping you up as you count.

CD Track 80

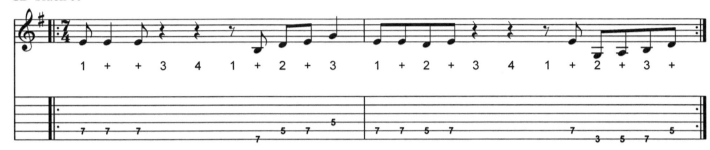

Pink Floyd's "Money" is a familiar example of 7/4 in the reverse grouping order (3 + 4).

Longer quarter-note-based odd meters (9/4, 11/4, etc.) and oddly-grouped even meters (8/4, 10/4) are possible, but they too should usually be counted in smaller pieces. Counting the full meter does not tell you where the accents are. For example, the intro to The Allman Brothers' "Whipping Post" in 11/4 is most easily counted as 3 + 3 + 3 + 2.

Odd Eighth-Note Meters

If eighth-note odd meters contain groups of two and three, and the tempo is too high to tap every eighth note, it's finally advisable to tap the foot differently within the same measure. This is the only time you should do this. We'll tap our foot once for **long beats** (three eighth notes) and once for **short beats** (two eighth notes) in these assymetrical meters. Practice slowly, speaking all the numbers as you tap the foot only on the first note of each group. Set the metronome to tick the eighth notes. Beware of blurring the long and short beats. Make sure you can still feel every eighth note in your body.

Here's an example in 5/8; one long beat, then a short one.

CD Track 81

Now we'll try one in 7/8, with one long, two shorts: 3 + 2 + 2.

CD Track 82

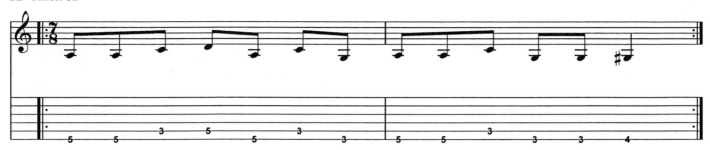

Some eighth-note meters contain odd groups but don't require irregular foot taps. For example, 8/8 can be grouped 123 123 12, just like the additive rhythm in Chapter 16. If the measure adds up to an even number of eighth notes, you might get better results by tapping even quarter notes, and syncopating your accents. If the tempo is high, you can tap your foot twice per bar for 2/2 or *cut time*. Each of these measures should sound the same. Only the foot tapping is different.

CD Track 83

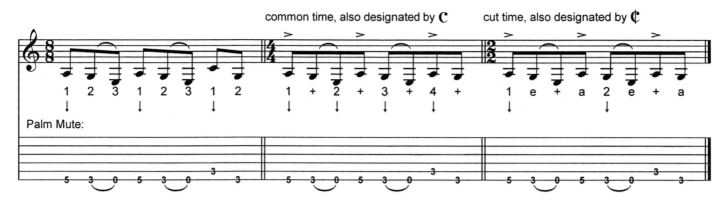

A 10/8 groove in the style of "Mission Impossible" is grouped 123 123 12 12 at the eighth-note level, but can be tapped in 5/4. Tapping in half time would cause the second half of the riff to be completely syncopated. Try it!

CD Track 84

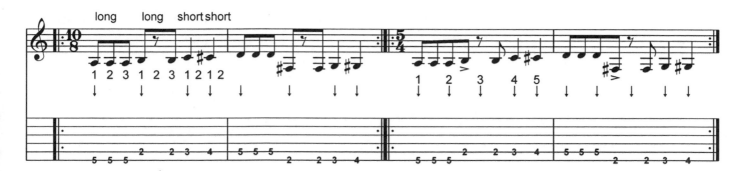

15/8 time looks scary but if there are five groups of three (check the beaming) you just have a 5/4 shuffle.

CD Track 85

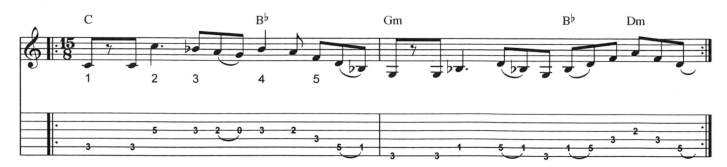

Write out odd-meter riffs, rhythm grooves, and melodies. Keep them simple at first so you can feel every downbeat. Work out motifs for them on paper and count them in correctly. Record more backing tracks like this chapter's practice assignment, and solo over them until your phrasing fits the meter to the point you forget that you're doing something out of the ordinary. You'll have a lot of fun learning, and your regular 4/4 chops will become more solid in the process.

For the Obsessed

Meters with 16 in the denominator are felt in the same way as the eighth- and quarter-note based meters above: in groups of twos, threes, or fours. They are written with the 16th note as the pulse for convenience; for example if a song starts with a 4/4 sixteenth-note funk groove, but later has a section where one sixteenth note is cut from each measure, it makes sense to write it as 15/16 so that it compares with the earlier material. This would be easier to understand than writing the new part in 15/8 and stating that the new eighth note is equal to the old sixteenth note.

Another method of counting meters with multiple odd groups at a small division level is to use the syllables "Ta ki ta" for threes and "Ta ka" for twos. For a measure of 13/8 or 13/16 you might repeat this, while tapping the foot on each "Ta":

```
Ta ki ta Ta ka Ta ki ta Ta ka Ta ki ta
1  2  3  1  2  1  2  3  1  2  1  2  3
```

You should know how to tap your foot and count for any meter, and to adapt to high tempos by tapping in half time, or grouping any three eighth notes into one beat. Go slowly when learning any new groove for the first time. OK, now I'm only going to say this once. If the tempo is insanely fast and the meter consists of irregularly ordered groups of 2s and 3s, it might be all right to play without tapping the foot. But make sure you still feel every beat and division in your body, and don't let me catch you.

Chapter 19: Displacements, Polyrhythms, and Metric Modulations

Previously we rhythmically-displaced short motifs to create interest within a phrase. Displacement of longer melodic phrases can let us play across bar lines, and the boundaries of phrases or sections, while keeping the meter and form.

Eighth-Note Displacement of a Riff

Here we'll play a riff twice, but start it an eighth note later the second time. It'll feel a little bit like a bar of 9/8 followed by one of 7/8, though the overall time is still two measures of 4/4. The first example contains the fewest possible notes to show how a full measure displacement works.

If everyone in the band plays the displacement, a casual listener who is tapping along in quarter notes will have to stop, listen, and start tapping again. If the drummer preserves the 4/4 feel, the displaced riff will just come across as syncopation against it. The two approaches are approximated with a drum machine on the CD.

CD Track 86

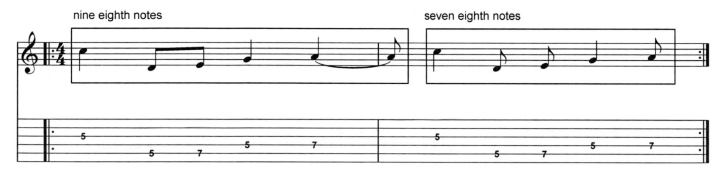

The effect is more pronounced when you add pickup notes and chord changes, and the extra time is inserted somewhere besides the end of the phrase. Here's the intro to "Welcome Your Overlords." An extra eighth note of time is added after the pickup.

CD Track 87

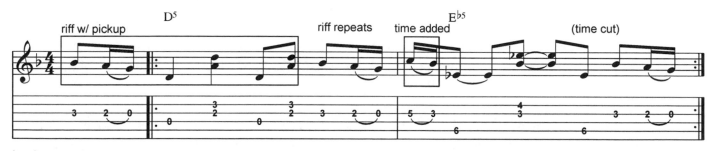

Assignment

Write a one-bar pentatonic riff similar to the first example above, but with a pickup going into the downbeat. Make sure the end of the riff has a space an eighth note longer than the pickup phrase, which you'll copy onto the same beat as before. Add one eighth note of time at the beginning of the second measure, then copy the riff, displaced by that one eighth note. Copy the pickup at the end of measure 2 so you can form a two-bar loop.

Count, learn, and practice the two riffs as if they had nothing to do with each other. When both are memorized, hook them together and play as a loop.

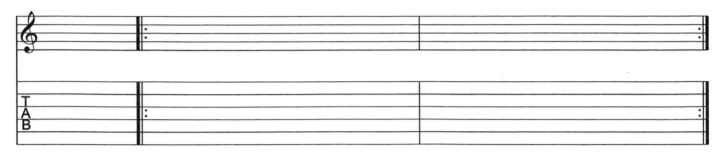

Quarter-Note Displacement

With displacement by a quarter note, the pulse stays the same but the perceived downbeat moves. In this example the pickup is displaced along with the rest of the riff.

CD Track 88

Songwriters usually reserve strong displacement for intros or interludes. Jimi Hendrix was especially interested in faking people out about where the downbeat was. *Band of Gypsys* has the riff to cop in "Power of Love" at 1:20 and 2:13. Also check out the intros to "Remember" on *Are You Experienced?* and "All Along the Watchtower" on *Electric Ladyland*.

We looked at displacement by an eighth note and by a quarter note, but you can try displacement in your song arrangements or solos by any amount: a sixteenth note, two-thirds of a triplet, a dotted quarter note, etc. If you want to keep the time signature intact, you must later subtract whatever you've added.

Assignment

Write a two-bar pentatonic riff like my example above. Use at least one pickup note. Make sure it finishes early enough to accommodate repetition. Displace it by a quarter note the second time.

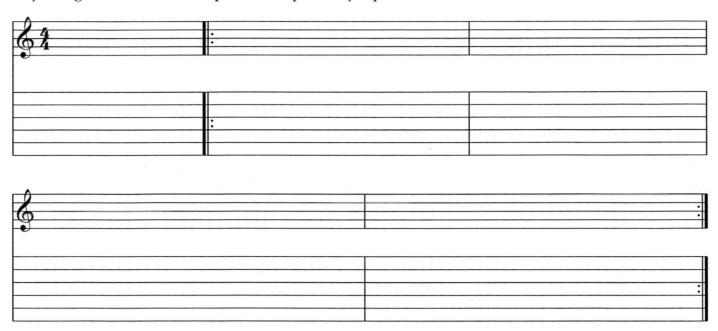

Polymetric Phrasing

This is not quite as hard as it sounds. A basic example is continuous repetition of a three-beat motif over a 4/4 groove. We're relying on the band to keep playing in 4/4 while we imply 3/4 in the solo. Unless you're a one-man act, you don't actually have to play in two different meters at once. It can be harder to transition back to the original meter than it is to break out with the new one, so have your exit figured out and practice it beforehand. Just like with additive rhythm sequences, once you know the new phrase it can usually be played while counting and tapping in the original meter.

Three-beat groups are labeled in this excerpt from "Mojito." The chord progression uses four-bar phrases. The original recording is in 2/2, but when practicing the example slowly, it's fine to count and tap in 4/4.

First the original meter is established with eighth notes for four measures, accenting each downbeat.

CD Track 89

Next a three-eighth-note-long rhythmic motif is repeated. Two of these motifs add up to match the ride cymbal pattern for a jazz waltz. The 3/4 figure creates a sense of tension and forward movement over the 4/4 underpinning. After four times on this figure we end up on the downbeat of bar 4 of this excerpt, then steady eighth notes resume to guide us back to the normal meter.

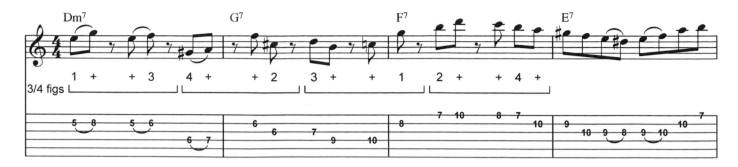

Single eighth-note pickups nailing beats 1 and 3 feel good after the previous rhythmic tension.

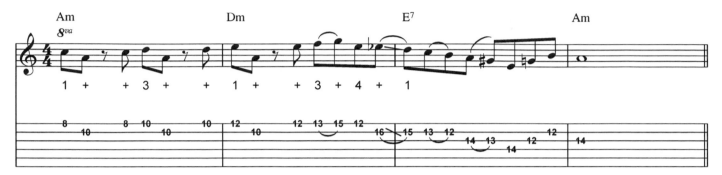

In this swing-feel example 3/4 overlays start in measure 1, beats 1 and 4, then happen three times starting on beat 3 of measure 5. As long as the duration of the figure is consistent, you can construct phrases to intensify or diminish the polymetric effect to your taste. I've used exactly the same lick three times to make it obvious here.

CD Track 90

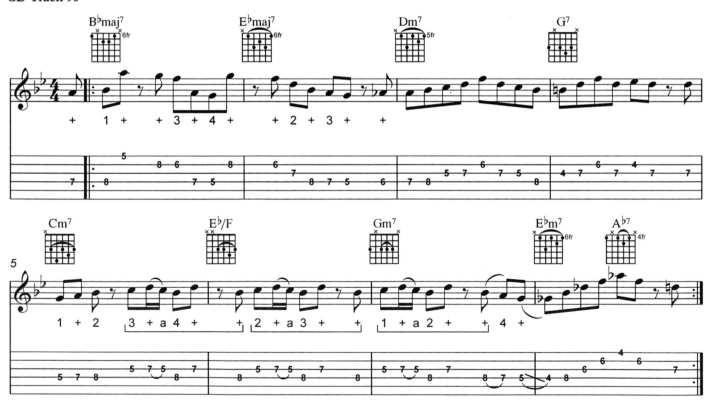

An easily-recognizable example of 3 over 4 polymeter in a rock composition is Zeppelin's "Kashmir," which maintains a continuous 3/4 figure over a 4/4 drum groove for its entire verse.

Calculating Resolutions

To find out how many repetitions it will take for a polymetric overlay to return to the beat it started on, you could write them all out, but there's another way. Find the lowest common multiple of a, the number of notes in its duration and b, the fraction of the measure that note represents. The lowest common multiple (LCM) is the smallest number that is divisible by both a and b, keeping in mind that any number is divisible by itself.

Let's say we have a five-quarter-note figure in 4/4 time. There are 5 quarter notes so $a = 5$. There are four quarter notes per bar in 4/4, so $b = 4$. The LCM of 5 and 4 is 20. The lick will come out after twenty quarter notes: five bars, or four repetitions of the lick. Here it starts on bar 2 and comes out on bar 7.

CD Track 91

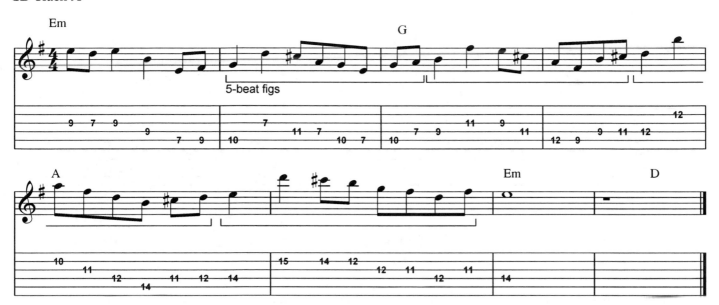

A four-eighth-note ($a = 4$) group in 12/8 time ($b = 12$) will come out after only 12 eighth notes (three reps), because the LCM of 4 and 12 is 12.

CD Track 91 cont'd.

We'll do one more just to confirm the math: a five-eighth note group in 9/8 time. The LCM of 5 and 9 is 45. The lick would come out after 45 eighth notes, which is five measures of 9/8, nine reps of the lick.

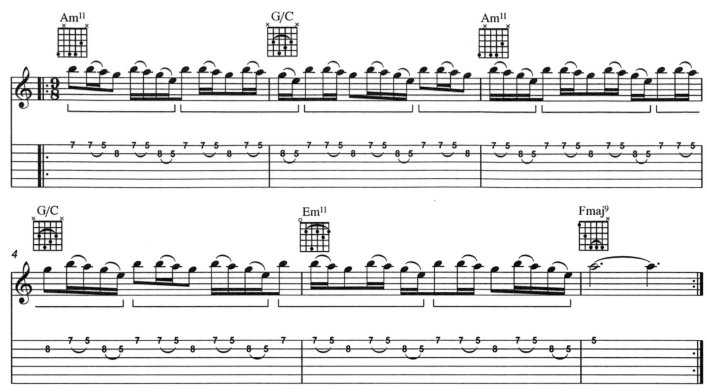

Exercise 7

Use the formula on the previous page to find out how many times a six-eighth-note figure that starts on beat 1 must be played in order to come out on a later downbeat in 4/4.

There's no law that says you have to continue a polymeter until downbeats converge. You can compose or improvise an exit after any number of repetitions. The real purpose of the above calculation, which brings you back to the same beat you started on, is to encourage you to think about time in a way you might not have before.

If you're the composer, you may decide not to return to the old meter or play both at once but to shift completely over to the new meter, which means you'll be creating a *metric modulation*.

Metric Modulation

This term is sometimes used as a name for polyrhythm or polymeter, but we'll use *modulation* to mean a change to a new meter for long enough that the old one is no longer felt. (It also applies to key changes.) These are not soloing phrasing ideas; they are rhythmic composition devices that we should be able to play and to solo over.

Any of these examples can be made easier by ignoring pitch and clapping out the rhythms only while tapping the pulse with your foot.

In the easiest meter changes, the foot taps the same pulse; you just count a different number of taps per bar. The downbeats are accented by melodic construct or dynamics.

You can hear a quarter-note meter change from 4/4 to 3/4 about 1 minute into the Beatles' "She Said, She Said."

You'd use the next type of meter change to keep the same pulse but go from a triplet-based feel to a straight one or vice versa. When the tempo stays the same, the equation is a *listesso* (Italian for *the same*). It tells you that the dotted quarter note in the old meter is equal to the quarter note in the new one. This kind of feel change happens in Freddie King's "Hideaway" at 1:49 and 2:09.

CD Track 93

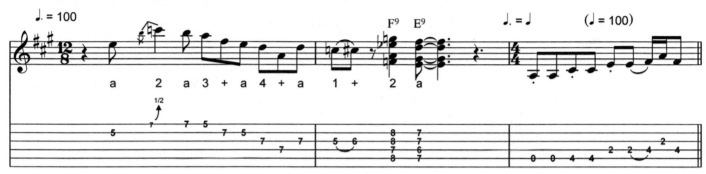

In a true or **pulse-changing** metric modulation, the result is a new tempo, created by using some calculable fraction of the previous beat. Here the eighth notes in 4/4 are regrouped in threes to create 6/8 time. If the eighth notes are the same duration (dictated by the metric equation), the new tempo will automatically be 66.6% of the old one. Your foot goes from tapping every other eighth note to one of every three.

CD Track 94

If you wanted to change to a three feel but make the tempo difference more drastic, you could have a measure of quarter note triplets from the original 4/4 meter become a bar of 6/8. The new tempo is 50% of the old.

CD Track 95

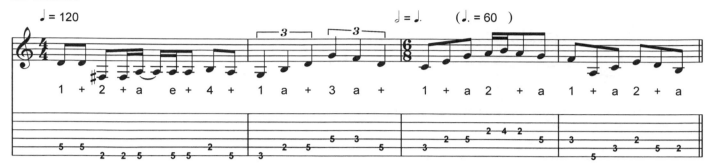

A modulation similar to the one above happens in the Beatles' "We Can Work It Out," at the end of each bridge.

To change the new groove back to the previous one, you could reverse the value indication, making the dotted quarter notes equal to half notes. It seems simple on paper, but to really nail it, we should work on the four over three feel separately. Let's do it with no pitch change; just working the rhythm. It'll be challenge enough if this is new for you.

To work with familiar figures, we'll switch from 6/8 to 3/4 so there are groups of two instead of three. Next, you can see four groups of three sixteenth notes, notated with dots and ties. These dotted eighth notes become the quarter notes in the original faster meter.

CD Track 96

You may also see the four-against-three written as an eighth-note quadruplet in 3/4 time. These two measures are the same.

Meter changes can be a good idea for bridges and solo sections in songs. Usually the change is abrupt, with everyone going to the new meter at once (a *direct* modulation), but it may be preceded by someone polymetrically superimposing the new meter over the old one (a *pivot* modulation).

In this direct metric modulation example from "Devil's House Party" the groove starts in 12/8, with three eighth notes per beat. The beat is a dotted quarter note. In the new meter, the eighth notes are the same length but now there are only two per foot-tap. The new groove is 150% faster as a result.

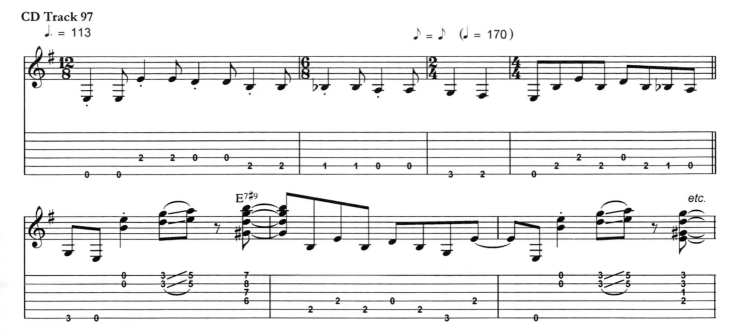

Tempo Changes

There is no requirement that a tempo change be dictated by a fractional relationship between pulses in different sections. Often the instruction is just to play faster or slower (possibly stated in Italian, German, or French), or to approximate a new metronome setting. If the tempo change is gradual, you will see *accelerando* or *ritardando*.

The band has to execute tempo changes together perfectly, so they're usually only wise to attempt if you have experienced players and sufficient rehearsal time. The drummer should be dictating the time, unless you're playing with a conductor, or to a click track that has been programmed to change.

Hard Stuff

At some point you may hear or conceive a rhythmic idea that is beyond your immediate capacity to play. It's also possible you may encounter a written rhythm that is too hard to read. For small notes mixed together with longer ones, we'll use augmentation. For rhythmic figures that obscure beats we're used to seeing or feeling, we'll break the notes into smaller parts and use ties to help show the beats.

Augmentation

If you have very small notes mixed with bigger ones, rewrite the part, doubling the duration of each note. What was a one-bar passage will now be two bars. Work it up to speed, eventually cutting the foot tapping back to the original pulse. If it is still too hard, you can expand it again, to four bars.

CD Track 98

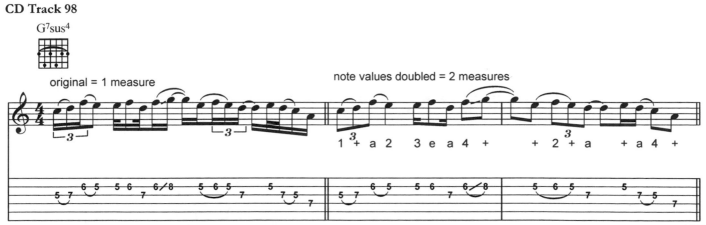

105

Breaking Rhythms Down to See the Beats

If you have a rhythm that crosses beats in a way that is hard to understand (meaning its notes are effectively too long) then a diminutive process (but not actual diminution) is called for where you break a large note into two that are half the size, then tie them together so that you can see where the attacks are in relation to the beat.

Suppose, for example, you have trouble feeling quarter-note triplets in 4/4. Write out two eighth-note triplets, marking the beats and divisions below. Then tie every other note, and emphasize the desired attacks while counting all the divisions. Keep that foot tapping the pulse.

To learn the half-note triplet, use the same process: write out two quarter-note triplets, and attack every other note.

CD Track 99

In my early teaching days I had a student ask me what it would sound like to displace an eighth-note triplet by an eighth note. He wrote something like this on the board.

CD Track 99 cont'd.

The above notation is not the best music copying practice. For another way to notate it, and find out what it sounds like, write two sixteenth-note triplets so that beat 2 is clearly visible, then attack every other note.

Now it's recognizable as a common rhythm. But if the tied sixteenth-note triplet shuffles are too hard to read, you can apply augmentation and spread the example out over two bars. Practice it over eight foot taps, speed it up, then play it over four.

CD Track 99 cont'd.

Conclusion

The purpose of this book has been to train your rhythmic sense, not to limit it. You may combine multiple phrases of various lengths, crossing bar lines and section boundaries, and start and end your phrases on any beat you like, but hopefully now with a solid awareness of where that downbeat is. Finding the amount of predictability you prefer in your style is up to you. In the listening public, there are fans of simplicity and order, freaks for complexity or chaos, and many appreciate it all.

With thoughtful practice you can learn to really know and feel what's ahead of you and what came before when soloing. Once the homework is done, you become free to stop worrying, follow your gut, and just play what feels right in the moment.

Appendix

The Fretboard

By placing the 1st finger successively on each C, at frets 1, 3, 5, 8, and 10, while at the same time reaching to the next C higher up the fretboard with the 3rd or 4th finger, we get five distinct overlapping **root shapes** for C. Each corresponds to a fret-hand position for scales, chords, or arpeggios. The five shapes for C start over at the13th fret, which you can see here as the second instance of pattern 1.

C Root Shapes

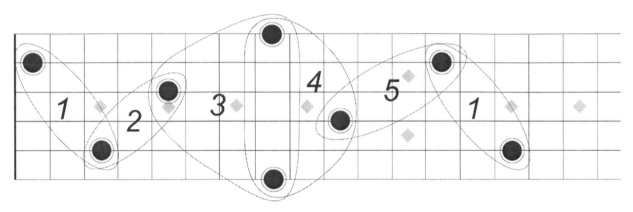

Root-shape patterns 3 and 4 (marked with irregular outlines) are the only adjacent patterns that share two roots, on the 6th and 1st strings.

Each shape corresponds to the roots of a familiar open-position chord, so many players refer to the successive shapes as forms C, A, G, E, and D of the CAGED system.

The five patterns of root shapes stay the same for all twelve unique pitches. For example, by moving each dot closer to the body by one fret, we get all instances of the pitch C♯ (or D♭), which is always a half step higher than C.

C♯ or D♭ Root Shapes

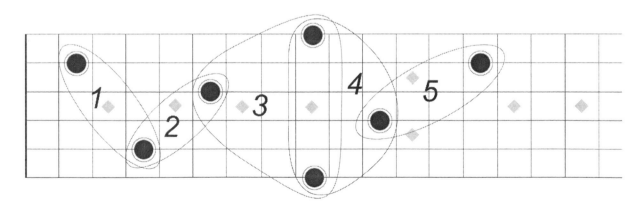

Moving them all up by another fret gives us the five root shapes for the note D natural, with Pattern 5 starting on the open D or 4th string.

D Root Shapes

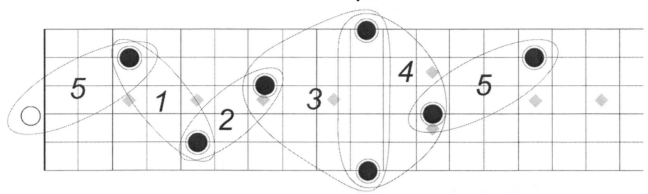

Play and memorize the five root shapes with their numbers. Describe them aloud as follows, but do not include specific fret numbers in your descriptions. Once learned they will help you find the notes on your instrument.

"Pattern 1, roots on strings 2 and 5, two frets apart."
"Pattern 2, roots on strings 5 and 3, two frets apart."
"Pattern 3, roots on strings 3, 6, and 1, three frets apart."
"Pattern 4, roots on strings 6, 1, and 4, two frets apart."
"Pattern 5, roots on strings 4 and 2, three frets apart."

For practice, move the notes in the previous diagram up by two frets to mark every E on this diagram, then circle and label the five root shapes. Include the open low and high E strings in pattern 4.

E Root Shapes

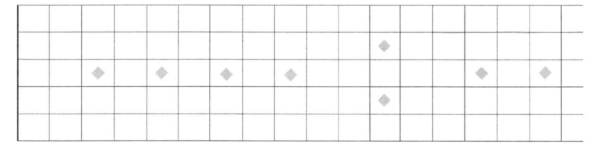

Mark every G note on this neck diagram, then circle and label the five patterns of root shapes. Include the open G string.

G Root Shapes

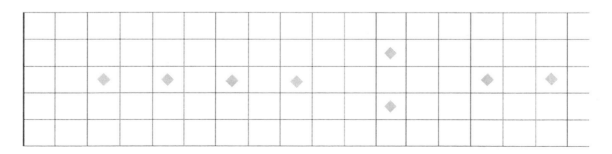

Positional Scales of the CAGED System

If you completely visualize a scale **before** you start playing it, you will learn it more easily, with fewer mistakes. Redraw the diagram on paper to help you memorize the pattern faster than you would by playing it over and over. Pay close attention to the circled root shapes. With these major scales, you'll want your 2nd finger on the root that is closest to the guitar's nut.

Major

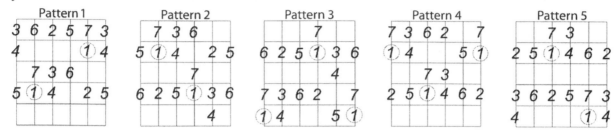

Major Pentatonic

These are the same as major, with degrees 4 and 7 removed.

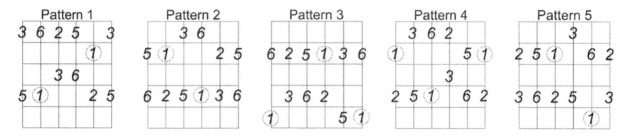

Minor

These are the same patterns as major scales starting from degree 6. The 6th degree of a major scale is the root of its relative minor.

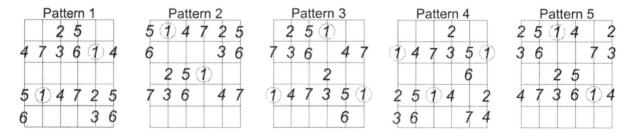

Minor Pentatonic

These are the same as minor, with degrees 2 and 6 removed.

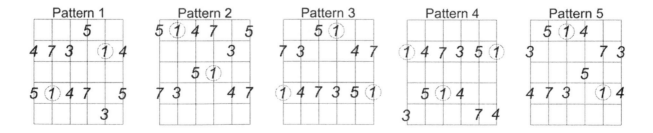

110

Arpeggios

An arpeggio is the tones of a chord played in any order separately rather than simultaneously. Play the corresponding triad (three-note) arpeggios by removing the 7th degree from each arpeggio below.

Major 7th (R-3-5-7)

The corresponding triad is major.

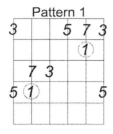
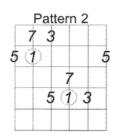

Minor 7th (R-♭3-5-♭7)

The corresponding triad is minor.

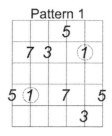
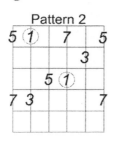
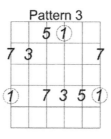
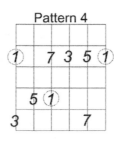
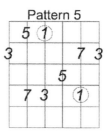

Dominant 7th (R-3-5-♭7)

The corresponding triad is major.

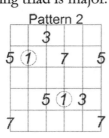
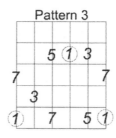
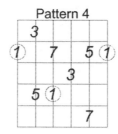
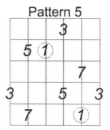

Minor 7♭5 (R-♭3-♭5-♭7)

The corresponding triad is *diminished*.

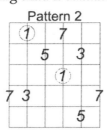
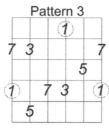
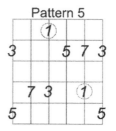

Diminished 7th (R-♭3-♭5-♭♭7)

Since all its notes are a minor third apart, diminished 7th arpeggio shapes are the same all over the fretboard. The corresponding triad is *diminished*. Removing the 7th produces slightly irregular shapes.

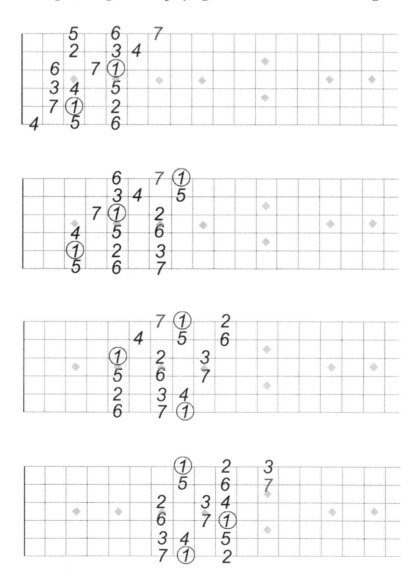

3-Note-Per-String Scales

Each of these moves from one positional root shape to another as it ascends. They are a bit harder to play through key and chord changes, but good for playing faster lines and connecting the fretboard.

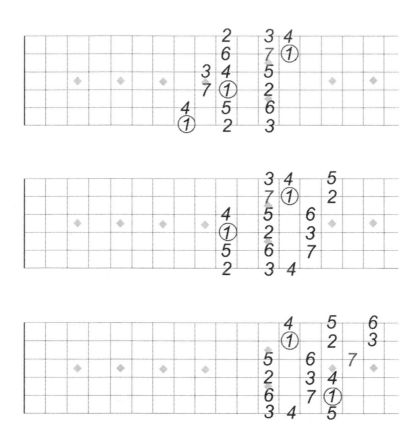

Modes

Any major scale pattern may be used to produce any of the seven major modes. The sound of the mode is produced by the harmonic context and the notes you choose to emphasize.

Number	Mode Name	Basic Quality	Spelling from its own root
1	Ionian	major	1 2 3 4 5 6 7
2	Dorian	minor	1 2 ♭3 4 5 6 ♭7
3	Phrygian	minor	1 ♭2 ♭3 4 5 ♭6 ♭7
4	Lydian	major	1 2 3 ♯4 5 6 7
5	Mixolydian	dominant	1 2 3 4 5 6 ♭7
6	Aeolian	minor	1 2 ♭3 4 5 ♭6 ♭7
7	Locrian	minor	1 ♭2 ♭3 4 ♭5 ♭6 ♭7

Rather than learn new fretboard patterns for modes 2 through 7, you can find and use the patterns of the related major scale for each. To find a mode correctly you must first know the major scale formula.

$$1\ 2\ 3^{\wedge}4\ 5\ 6\ 7^{\wedge}8$$

There are half steps from 3-4 and from 7-8. A half step is a one-fret distance. Between all the other notes are whole steps. A whole step is a two-fret distance on the same string.

You must also know that there are naturally-occurring half steps from B to C and from E to F in the musical alphabet. All other natural notes are whole steps apart.

$$A\ B^{\wedge}C\ D\ E^{\wedge}\ F\ G\ A$$

To get the mode D Dorian you would declare D the 2nd degree in a major scale. Following the major scale formula, count down to find the Ionian. In this example we only need to remember there is a whole step from 2 to 1 in the major scale. We find that the Ionian is C.

2   D
1   C

You'd play any C major scale pattern, but resolve phrases on the note D, and you would do this over a D minor chord.

Let's do that again with another mode. To get F Mixolydian, remember the mode number (5). Declare F the 5 of a major scale and count down.

5   F
4   E♭
3   D
2   C
1   B♭

We have declared F is degree 5. From 5 to 4 is a whole step, which means the next note in the countdown is E♭. This is because the distance from F to E is a natural half step. Continuing down the major scale formula, we see a half step from E♭ to D, so the D doesn't need an accidental. Continuing with the other steps, we find B♭ is the Ionian. We'd play the B♭ major scale to get F Mixolydian, only we'd phrase to the note F. We'd play this over an F major triad or F dominant 7th chord.

One more example; students need to do this many times before the process is fast enough to apply in action. To get G Lydian, we remember the mode number (4). Declare G the 4th degree, and count down to find the Ionian.

4   G
3   F♯
2   E
1   D

You'd play D major, phrasing to G, to get G Lydian. You'd play this mode over a G major triad or a Gmaj7 chord.

Now you try it. It's worth the effort because your major scale patterns will become more useful in real playing.

Exercise 8
Use the above method to find the Ionian for the following modes.

F# Aeolian
A Phrygian
D Locrian
G♭ Lydian
E♭ Mixolydian

Answers to Exercises

Exercise 1 (p. 49)

Track	Beat Division	Feel
51	eighth note	straight
62	sixteenth note	straight
67	sixteenth note	shuffle

Exercise 4 (p. 55)

Track	Phrase Length
51	4 bars
62	2 bars
73	4 bars

Exercise 7 (p. 102)

The LCM of 6 and 8 is 24. You will come out on a downbeat after 24 eighth notes, which is 3 measures or 4 repetitions of the figure.

Exercise 8 (p. 114)

F$\sharp$ Aeolian	=	A Ionian
A Phrygian	=	F Ionian
D Locrian	=	E$\flat$ Ionian
G$\flat$ Lydian	=	D$\flat$ Ionian
E$\flat$ Mixolydian	=	A$\flat$ Ionian

CPSIA information can be obtained at www.ICGtesting.com
Printed in the USA
LVOW091327190812

294977LV00001B/6/P